Neighbor to Adirondack Wilderness: Howard Zahniser's "Mateskared Cabin"

By Ed Zahniser

Mountain light condenses to evening clouds
Wind comes and suddenly blows them apart
May I inquire of people in the mountains,
What's it like looking out of the mountains?
— Shi Jian, transl. Steven Allee

Indoor fireplace and mantel beam in Mateskared Cabin by Karen Z. Bettacchi

Neighbor to Adirondack Wilderness:
Howard Zahniser's "Mateskared Cabin"

by Ed Zahniser

ISBN: 978-0-9701664-7-0

Copyright © 2023 Ed Zahniser

All Rights Reserved
No part of this book may be reproduced or transmitted in any form whatesoever without prior written permission from the publisher except in the case of a brief quotation embodied in critical articles and reviews

Cover Photo: Don Rittner
Back Cover: Justin Duewel-Zahniser

Published by Warren County Historical Society
50 Gurney Lane
Queensbury NY, 12084
www.wcnyhs.org

Foreword

Historian and Adirondack Mountains poet Ed Zahniser has been my guide to the roots of Wilderness philosophy and history for more than three decades. With *Neighbor to Adirondack Wilderness*, he shares his humble wisdom with readers and admirers from across the country. His latest prose collection reminds us to think more deeply about our own home places, those places on Earth where we feel most grounded in life.

Ed's stories reflect his life growing up as the younger son of the Federal 1964 Wilderness Act author Howard Zahniser. They also transcend his own life to trace the history of American Transcendentalism, from Ralph Waldo Emerson, Henry David Thoreau, to his father, Howard. Now, Ed has become a grandfather, sharing with his readers the practical, deeply felt realities of growing up and gaining comfort and courage as a neighbor to wild forests, wild winds, wild scents, wildlife and wildness.

Do you, the reader, wish to feel more familiar, more at home with "the wolf" and other wild nature that resides both within you and me and, perhaps, as your nearest neighbor beyond your fence line? Do you want to know more about the concepts and the history of Wilderness preservation in the Adirondacks and across America? Then, read on. This is a book to savor at a leisurely Adirondack pace, as though you are walking down a long, winding forest trail towards the western sunset, not bounded by calls, ticking, tweets, or notifications on your Apple watch. Each story can be enjoyed and read on its own, or as a continuum.

Ed's stories reveal a poet, a philosopher, a father, and a wilderness historian. He grew up in an extended Zahniser family of ministers to human souls. His father Howard tailored that ministerial tradition to satisfy the deep need in our human souls to restore ourselves in wild places. In wilderness, our human influences do not dominate the land. Instead, we exercise the humility to know all that we do not know about how the greater community of life around us truly works. And we perceive the extent of our destruction when we wrongly assume we do know how it all works. Through Ed's Adirondack memories and lessons, we learn that wilderness is less natural resource management and more the practice of human restraint on ecosystems we still know far too little about.

In *Neighbor to Adirondack Wilderness*, Ed Zahniser locates his family's 20th-century wilderness knowledge—that we are dependent members of an interdependent community of life that gains its energy from the Sun (quoting his father)—in the context of his family's second-home place. Ed feels most grounded in New York's Adirondack Park, in the Town of Johnsburg, Warren County. Here, his father worked on drafting the National Wilderness Preservation System Act of

1964. It is grounded in New York's Adirondacks and "forever wild" State Constitution—wild by law, not by administrative whim.

Ed's neighbor since he was one year old is now 114,000 acres of designated, public, Siamese Ponds Wilderness. His Adirondack mentor and neighbor was the late, great Adirondack wilderness advocate Paul Schaefer. Schaefer deeply influenced Howard Zahniser in wilderness campaigning and overcoming the notion deeply embedded in our nation's cultural history, that wilderness is antithetical to American economic "progress." In reading these stories, you come face to face with the daily, practical, and philosophical reasons why that notion no longer serves us. Ed reminds us that Wilderness protection anticipated and remains at the core of all of the environmentalism necessary to restore our life support systems — our forests, our oceans, our very climate —on planet earth.

Before we are wilderness advocates, we must practice daily life as the daughters, sons, mothers, fathers, fishers, campers, lovers, and teachers of others. First, we must sense being part of a community, the entire community of life around us. We must feel more comfortable and more sociable with the wild, in the wild, and with those growing up as neighbors of the wild. In Ed's case, this was the people of the Adirondacks. How do we do all this? Read on.

You, too, are part of this story. You, too, are taking steps, teaching your children, and making history. Ed Zahniser is one of our guides. His stories point us toward the ultimate realization of our interdependency with the more than human world. Broaden your own horizons and enjoy Ed's down to earth philosophy. Be Wild. Read on.

David Gibson, Managing Partner
Adirondack Wild: Friends of the Forest Preserve

Table of Contents

Foreward, 1
New York State's Wilderness Estate, 5
Where the Wilderness Begins, 9
Howard Zahniser and The Black River Wars, 13
The Waters of Wildness, 19
Paul Schaefer: The Glue for New York State Wilderness, 23
The Whole Scheme of Life, 27
Howard Zahniser's Culture Heroes, 31
'There Is A Wolf in Me!', 35
Ducks on Carps' Backs, Walking, 39
Mateskared's Builders and First Inhabitants, 43
Tapping into the Spring, 47
Letters of "Bobcat" Ranney and Howard Zahniser, 51
The Oehser Camp and Fred West, 57
Porcupine Deconstructs Landscape Art, 63
The Cellar and Past Neighbors Uphill, 65
Fence Full of Car Parts in Bakers Mills, 69
Part of Your Barn Is on Me', 71
What Hugh Lackey Told Paul Schaefer, 73
Cabin as Nesting and Well-being, 77
"Cabin in the Mountains", 81
Celestial Burial and Other Cabin Chores, 83
Honeymoon Delayed but Prolonged, 87
Cabin Yard: Acting Rock and Steamboat Rock, 91
Echo Park: Prelude to the Wilderness Act, 93
From Yard Rocks to Big Rock, 97
Big Rock, 99

Early Morning on the Cabin Porch, 101

Our Spring vs. Fossil Water, 105
My First Trout and 'The Rainmakers', 107
'Gotcha One Donut!', 111
Cub Schaefer and the Bull, 113
High Peaks in Blowdown, 121
Canon Cook, The Mother, 125
Paul Schaefer's Headwaters Faith, 127

Let Sleeping Cabins Lie, 131

The Ice Meadows, 133
Hooper Mine, 137
What Crane Mountain Said, 141
Crane Mountain from the Cabin Porch, 145
Bashô Walks Onward, 147

The Language of Life and Death, 149

Cowshed Dreaming, 153
Ant Lions, Sand, Anthropic Cosmological Principle, 155
Wilderness Act 50th Anniversary, 159
Coda: The Scale of Our Desires -Wholly Holy, 163
Lilac Time, 165
The World, Beauty, Pattern, and Order, 169
Epiloque: Reciprocity, by David Abram, 175

Note: The three free-standing italic entries in the Table of Contents below represent supposed monologues with our two sons, who were then on the cusp of their teen years as this material was being written.

New York State's Wilderness Estate

Why do precisely these objects which we behold make a world?
—Henry David Thoreau

Paul Oehser, my father Howard's friend from college days, once joked that "You've never experienced wilderness until you've driven through Iowa on Interstate 70 in a heavy rainstorm!" The former Chief of Publications at The Smithsonian Institution, Oehser was on his way to attend an annual meeting of The Wilderness Society governing council in Grand Junction, Colorado. His quip reveals one of many connotations of the inextricably entwined words *wilderness* and *wildness*.

Oehser's use of *wilderness* to evoke chaos harks back to Europe as cities came to be high earthly expressions of order, even divine order. Think Augustine of Hippo's tome *The City of God.* By contrast, wilderness was unordered landscape then. It lay outside the pale of the order brought by the Creator's chief agent, humankind. Watch the news today and modern unordered wilds seem to be big cities. Cities' often chaotic human disorders make the wilds of the Adirondack High Peaks or Moose River Plain look like environments of cooperation and restoration.

Wilderness became a personal and professional obsession for my father Howard Zahniser. He summed up lexical talk about wilderness with a carefully mixed metaphor: "Wilderness is where the hand of man has never set foot." Or Zahnie, as he was known, might say that "Wilderness is like virginity. It is defined by what you don't do."

Paul Schaefer, the great 20th-century Adirondack wilderness champion, remembered that Zahnie once so-defined wilderness for a group of dam proponents, including New York State legislators and State fish and game officials in the mid-1940s. The Black River Regulating District Board had called the meeting. The subject was the proposed Panther Mountain Dam that threatened to obliterate lowlands wilderness of the western Adirondacks. At issue were "forever wild" Forest Preserve lands protected as such by the New York State Constitution. Those lowland areas were also crucial wintering grounds for deer during the difficult winters.

Just before Zahnie's remarks, Adirondack guide and conservationist Ed Richards presented 200,000 signatures on petitions against the dam. But the law did not require the Regulating District Board to consider public sentiment, and the Board did not. Such was often the case for wilderness issues in the early 1950s.

Nevertheless, as Paul Schaefer later loved to point out, "Panther Mountain Dam was defeated by more than one million votes in a public referendum shortly thereafter."

Today, New York State boasts more officially designated state wilderness acreage than designated federal wilderness acreage. That fact has a rich history. New York law did not use the term *wilderness* for eighty years, but the Empire State beat the feds to the punch by holding state lands "forever wild," starting in the late 1800s. What is more, these lands were to be preserved as such in perpetuity under the state constitution—not by administrative whims of state conservation officials. This distinction would also be the central intent of the federal Wilderness Act of 1964: wild by law, not by administrative whim.

Zahnie would be the primary author of and chief lobbyist for the National Wilderness Preservation System Act of 1964. He also played a strong role in the wilderness battles for the integrity of New York State's Adirondack and Catskill Forest Preserve lands in the 1940s and 1950s. In his book *Cabin Country*, Paul Schaefer wrote that "Zahniser added national pressure through the Wilderness Society and other national groups." In the thick of the fray in 1948, Paul had written that ". . . Zahniser and his [Wilderness] Society have left no stone unturned that might aid New Yorkers in maintaining their Forest Preserve inviolate." Zahnie brought eight national conservation groups to those Adirondack wilderness controversies. In 1972, New York created its own wilderness system, adopting the definition of wilderness Zahnie devised for the 1964 Wilderness Act.

Zahnie shepherded the federal wilderness legislation through 66 revisions and 19 public hearings over the eight-year push for the law. He worked on several of those drafts at his desk in our family's Adirondack cabin. Until the late 1900s, our cabin was separated from the 17,000-acre Siamese Ponds Wilderness Area only by land that Paul Schaefer partly owned.

Schaefer and Zahnie first met in early 1946 in the wild canyons of New York City, at the Hotel Pennsylvania. Seven months earlier, Zahnie had left his secure federal government employment to become executive secretary and editor of the fledgling group, The Wilderness Society. The Society was formed in 1935 through the aegis of Robert Marshall, who cut his wilderness eye-teeth in the Adirondacks. Zahnie, then working for the U.S. Bureau of Biological Survey, became a charter member.

Marshall was a forestry scientist, author, explorer of Alaska's Brooks Range, and federal public lands bureaucrat. John Muir founded The Sierra Club, and his name is synonymous with Sierra Nevada wildlands, but Bob Marshall has come to personify American wilderness preservation. The Bob Marshall Wilderness Area in Montana is now affectionately known as "the Bob."

Too often overlooked, however, is that Bob Marshall was a second-generation wilderness advocate. His father, eminent jurist Louis Marshall of New York City, led the floor fight to defend the "forever wild" clause at the 1915 New York State Constitutional Convention. At the 1894 Convention, he had voted for this provision the "forever wild" clause," which today is Article XIV, Section 1:

"The lands of the state, now owned or hereafter acquired, constituting the forest preserve as now fixed by law, shall be forever kept as wild forest lands. They shall not be leased, sold or exchanged, or be taken by any corporation, public or private, nor shall the timber thereon be sold, removed or destroyed."

Wilderness is in fact, as Zahnie had quipped, defined by what you don't do. Unfortunately, a concerted constituency ever lurks, ever eager to do those things to and with wilderness that would make it cease to be wilderness. As national wilderness champion David Brower later asserted: "When they win, it's forever. When we win, it's merely a stay of execution."

Today, from the porch of our family cabin, you can look out onto designated wilderness on Eleventh Mountain, part of the New York State Siamese Ponds Wilderness Area. You can also look down the valley to wildlands of the state forest preserve on Crane Mountain. Which has changed more in the past sixty years, designated wilderness on trail-free Eleventh Mountain or Crane's forest preserve land, with its trails, popular pond, and expansive summit views?

The short answer might be "Crane," given increased human use since the 1950s and removal of the summit fire tower. A longer answer might be "probably Eleventh," given forest recovery, and changes afoot in the *concept* of wilderness and wildlands today.

Major physical change on Eleventh might be the small landslide in the 1990s. Also, with forest recovery—parts of the mountain were logged—trees are now much taller. Local resident the late Earl Allen once pointed out a new but continuing die-off of hardwoods. You could best see it from Edwards Hill Road out of Bakers Mills as lower-angled morning light splayed across the mountain. Human use on our spur of Eleventh is no doubt lower now, including in hunting and fishing seasons, than anyone now living might recall.

The late Grandma Annie Hitchcock called her neighbor the mountain "Old Number Eleven." Indeed, an old map with hachure lines to indicate the mountain's topography labels it "Number Eleven." State land surveyors had grown tired of rooting out local names or making up names. Annie Hitchcock would also personify the mountain to report how fall winds greatly reduced its foliage. "Number Eleven blew off last night," she would report.

Wilderness thinking anticipated our contemporary environmental concerns for natural systems and processes. In his speeches about wilderness, Zahnie would point out that the word *wilderness* ends with the suffix *-ness,* which denotes a quality. Wilderness is not so much a place or resource as a qualitative condition. This seed of thinking about wilderness not as real estate but as a condition—wilderness character, wildness—that inheres in the land and waters and flora and fauna has been in the background all along.

When Adirondack wilderness areas were designated by the State in the 1970s, the impetus was to protect certain lands from practices that would destroy their wilderness values. What New Yorkers were protecting is an entire regime of processes, many of which we probably have not yet even identified or do not yet understand. The *-ness* of *wilderness* connotes not a thing but qualities of working and interrelating. Wilderness statutes, state and federal, specifically intend to protect wildlands' ability to proceed by their own inherent dictates.

This requires constant citizen advocacy, however, as 2016 plans to motorize and mechanize vast chunks of the Essex Chain Lakes starkly revealed. Current law held those lands off-limits to motorized and mechanized activities. The announced Adirondack Park Agency (APA) and Department of Environmental Conservation (DENCON) plan also would have usurped the State Legislature's prerogative by changing the law absent legislative action. The APA and DENCON plan would also have obliterated a wilderness future for 40 designated primitive areas that current law specifically protected in anticipation of their wilderness futures.

Administrators were once again bent on wrestling wilderness away from its protection by law. In the process, they also threatened the state constitution's express intent to protect Adirondack Park Forest Preserve lands in perpetuity, "forever wild."

Where the Wilderness Begins

". . . in all traditional cultures, the habitation possesses a sacred aspect by the simple fact that it reflects the world.
— Mircea Eliade

My father and mother, Howard and Alice Zahniser, named our cabin *Mateskared* not long after they bought the place in late August 1946 from Harold and Pansy Allen. It sits at the end of Edwards Hill Road, off Route 8 in Bakers Mills, Town of Johnsburg, Warren County, New York.

The late great New York State conservationist Paul Schaefer was part owner of the land just across the dirt road that now ends at our place. Paul served as middleman on the deal because our family lived in the Washington, D.C., suburbs. We were a two-day drive from the Adirondack State Park in those days. I was not yet one year old.

When the deal went through, Paul, who had first invited our family to the Adirondacks earlier that summer, composed and sent my parents this telegram:

"Yours are the woods, waters, and wildlife of an Adirondack cabinland—up at the end of the trail where the wilderness begins, where a long peaceful valley meets the rocky buttresses of Crane and a sea of peaks rolls on to a far horizon. May you always cherish these rough untillable acres as a wild deer loves a sunny mountain ledge or an eagle the boundless reaches of sky."

Paul and my father, who was known as Zahnie, both loved words. *Mateskared* is composed of the first syllables of the names of the four children in our family, in birth order: *Mat*hias, *Es*ther, *Kar*en, and *Ed*ward.

"Is that an Indian name?" people sometimes ask? Well, it's fully as Indian as many Indian names bandied about the American scene.

As in most things Adirondack, Zahnie took the naming notion from Paul Schaefer. Paul's late parents' summer camp lies down the hill and across the road. It is named *Cragorehol*, from the first syllables of nearby mountains' names: *Cra*ne, *Gor*e, *E*leventh, and *H*eight *o*f *L*and. Children of Paul's late sister Gertrude Fogarty now own *Cragorehol*.

In 1946, our hillside plot was still subsistence farmland. Paul Schaefer's finely wrought telegram described it as "where the wilderness begins"—nature— and as "these rough, untillable acres"—culture. Indeed, it was agri-culture attempted in the brevity we know as human time. Both qualities of *Mateskared*, the natural and the cultural, ring true these many decades since my parents implanted this cabinland in our family story.

My father borrowed the money to buy *Mateskared* in August 1946 from the bank in Washington, D.C., that already held a mortgage, initiated in 1943, on our family home. We lived in what was then the relatively far-out northwest Washington, D.C. suburb of Hyattsville, Maryland. To make fiscal matters even less likely, my father had left a secure management job with the federal government in late September 1945. He had taken a cut in pay and veritable erasure of benefits to go to work for The Wilderness Society. The Society, a fledgling wildlands conservation outfit then, had been organized around Adirondacker Robert "Bob" Marshall in 1935.

When Zahnie changed jobs, my mother Alice was pregnant with me, their fourth child. I was to be birthed in The Wilderness Society milieu. Questioned about my father's leaving federal employment for a fledgling group with a fringe interest, my mother said she told him he should do whatever made him happy.

I can't imagine the word *collateral* even coming up in the conversation between my father and his banker about a second-home loan—especially if the banker were at all compassionate.

"Oh, you're not with the Agriculture department anymore?"

"No, I'm now the executive secretary of The Wilderness Society and editor of its quarterly magazine, *The Living Wilderness*."

"The Wilderness Society. . . what is that?"

"It's the national conservation organization founded in 1935 by millionaire philanthropist Robert Marshall." (*National* meant its members lived in several states; *millionaire* did *not* mean that Bob Marshall, who had died in 1939, left *all* his money to The Wilderness Society.)

"*Con-ver-SA-tion* organization?"

"No, sir, *con-ser-VA-tion* organization."

Their conver*sa*tion about conser*va*tion—Zahnie was to enunciate and explain that distinction many times in his early wilderness advocacy career—then switched to a show-and-tell event.

Zahnie pulled out a road map of New York State and the U.S. Geological Survey topographic quadrangle map for the Thirteenth Lake area of New York's massive Adirondack State Park. He also produced black-and-white photographs of the cabin and the view—of Crane Mountain—photographed from above and right below the cabin. He impressed on the banker how accessible the property was to New York City, the most populous area in these United States: location, location, location.

New to The Wilderness Society, Zahnie was effectively in on-the-job training to become, ten years later, the architect and chief lobbyist for the drive for national wilderness preservation legislation that would culminate in federal law, The National Wilderness Preservation System Act of 1964. This lobbying effort would require eight years. Much of that effort would take place just several blocks from my father's Washington, D.C. bank.

What my father and mother both had in common with *Mateskared* was that they too had grown up substantially off the money economy. My parents' families had not been subsistence farmers, however. Both of my grandfathers had been fervent, but, unsalaried, or minimally salaried, ministers, laborers in the vineyards of evangelical Christianity. My father's father was for much of his career paid in kind, in contributions of food and clothing, when there were enough for parishioners to share with them.

By 1946, my father had 15 years of experience in print and broadcast public relations and editing and writing. Now, he was in training to be a surprisingly successful organizer and lobbyist for a little-known and apparently anti-economic cause, wilderness preservation. The cause merely called into question the Great American Idea of Progress. But Zahnie had grown up in a household committed both physically and metaphysically to witnessing daily to other souls.

I'm surprised the banker didn't lend my father the *Mateskared* purchase money out of his own pocket.

Mateskared Cabin. Photo by Dave Gibson

Howard Zahniser in the Selway Bitterroot Wilderness Area, Montana, late 1950, by James Marshall, brother of Robert Marshall. Made during an annual meeting of The Wilderness Society governing council. It was a full-page feature in LIFE Magazine. Couretesy the Zahniser family.

Howard Zahniser and The Black River Wars

Howard Zahniser photo by Ed Zahniser

*"To know wilderness is to know a profound humility,
to recognize one's littleness, to sense dependence
and interdependence, indebtedness, and responsibility."
— Howard Zahniser*

Howard Zahniser knew he needed two things when he came to the Adirondacks in 1946. The two things could help him prove himself to his national wilderness mentors—now his recent employers—at The Wilderness Society. They could also help him build the practical and functional organization needed to pursue a national wilderness preservation system. First, Zahnie needed honest-to-goodness wilderness within reasonable automobile vacation reach of Washington, D.C. for our family of six. Second, he needed to expand his comfort zone of public relations, public information, and journalism work. He needed to learn grassroots political organizing and consensus building. He needed to learn to operate in the larger world that became the environmental movement 25 years later.

The Adirondacks and their Edwards Hill setting—soon to be Mateskared—met the first need. Paul Schaefer met the second. Paul was my father's ticket out of his own comfort zone.

Paul's longtime colleague Richard Messmer of the Friends of the Forest Preserve has said that Paul "was a master of consensus building" who "knew how to compromise, but not on principles." Paul's wide-ranging consensus building, genius for compromise, energy, dedication, attention to detail, and simple, beautifully articulated vision were "rarely found in a single individual," Messmer writes. "These characteristics and watching Paul in action, listening and learning from his great wisdom—made him a true mentor to many."

I doubt that anyone proved more attentive to Paul's promptings than Zahnie did in their early associations. Born in late 1945, I was too young to soak up directly the meanings of those early years in the 1940s and early 1950s. It would be many years after my father's death in 1964 before I began to see clearly the true dynamics of Paul's and Zahnie's early work together.

The Wilderness Society papers are lodged in the Conservation Library Center of the Denver Public Library. They show that some members of the Wilderness Society's governing board were not convinced that Zahnie was the right hire for executive secretary in 1945. Several thought Zahnie would not make substantive contributions to wilderness thought. Zahnie was hired for his publicity, journalistic, and office management skills. Those were crucially important functions for The Wilderness Society then, if only because Zahnie was the Society's only full-time staff member.

His resume to that point showed public relations editing, writing, and broadcasting. He had managed publicity for the Victory Garden Campaign in World War II. Founded in 1935, the young Society greatly needed to expand as a public membership organization. This would be crucial to building the constituency needed to pursue some type of national, legislated protection for wilderness areas on federal public lands. By design, The Wilderness Society had started out more like an advocacy think tank or learned society, not a broad-based membership organization. Nor was it clear in 1945 *how* federal wilderness areas should be protected. Zahnie was soon to have his first-ever experience of the Adirondacks and conservation political action—at Paul Schaefer's invitation.

Paul Schaefer lured Howard Zahniser to the Adirondacks in 1946 to help fight what became known as the Black River Wars. This eleven-year battle sought to save the Moose River Plains from a series of dam proposals. In the thick of the struggle, Paul wrote that it was the biggest Adirondack conservation battle of the 1900s. He reiterated that assessment in the late 1980s in his book *Defending the Wilderness*. I don't think Paul would have revised it even in the 1990s, after fifty years and lots more conservation battles. The controversy over the dams definitely surfaced Paul as a conservation leader in New York State. Paul jumped into what was then seen as a lost cause. He was to stick with it to the eventual reversal of the dam schemes—which involved a United States Supreme Court ruling.

The Black River Wars would prove to be a regional training ground for the early 1950s Echo Park dam proposal, a controversy over Dinosaur National Monument, a National Park Service area in Utah. In turn, the Echo Park fight—

several historians deem it the most important conservation battle of the 1900s—prepped the eight-year campaign for what became the federal 1964 Wilderness Act. Paul Schaefer and Mateskared figure in that progression of events.

Adirondack Cabin Country recounts an early-1950s visit Zahnie paid to Paul's old log cabin from Mateskared one summer afternoon. The purpose of their visit was to continue a conversation begun the night before up at Mateskared. Zahnie "was helping us develop national strategies for our battle to save the Moose River wilderness and its virgin forest located about 40 miles to the west," Paul wrote. "Because we had talked so long into the night, I asked him if he would rather take a hike into Bog Meadow. He agreed and we head for the trail that enters the Siamese Ponds wilderness." Later, Paul wrote "We are in no hurry. For me to be with Zahnie in wilderness is an end in itself, as I had discovered about five years earlier on our first trip into the Adirondack High Peaks. All of nature seems to take on a new significance when I walk leisurely with him in this kind of country."

That is Paul Schaefer reminiscing in the 1990s, by which time Paul's perception of their comparative status had shifted. That shift occurred before I was a teenager and spent great blocks of time with Paul. For many years, it prevented my grasping how formative Paul Schaefer and the Black River War campaign had been for Zahnie's early conservation career.

Paul picks up his reminiscing a few paragraphs later: "Howard is to leave for Washington tomorrow, so we review again our strategy for the Moose River fight, which after five years is reaching new legal and political heights. We talk about that greatest of conservation-minded families in New York: Louis, Jim, Bob, and George Marshall. We talk about Robert Sterling Yard, Richard Westwood, and Hugh Hammond Bennett. About Ira Gabrielson, Anthony Wayne Smith, and Pink Gutermuth, all of whom are involved in our New York conservation battles."

Paul's 1990s reminiscences do show Zahnie's arguably greatest contribution to the Black River Wars. When Zahnie jumped in it was a New York State controversy. Zahnie transformed it into a national conservation issue. Zahnie recruited Westwood, Gabrielson, Smith, and Gutermuth—all national conservation leaders—to defend the Moose River Plains. They and others Paul does not list here traveled to New York State. They gave influential expert testimony about the wilderness qualities and values of these "forever wild" Adirondack lands—Bob Marshall's country.

What Paul's 1990s reminiscences do *not* show was recorded in an article he wrote at the end of the Moose River fray. Written for a 1955 brochure for the conservation group Friends of the Forest Preserve, now Adirondack Wild: Friends of the Forest Preserve, the piece is reprinted in *Defending the Wilderness*: "Traveling became a way of life, with business responsibilities for many put in the background," Paul recorded. "New York City, Buffalo, Rochester, Syracuse, Utica, Binghamton, Kingston, Morrisville, Brownsville, Broadalbin, Cobleskill, Albany, Jamestown, Waverly. And hundreds more cities and towns. Movies and slides to overflow audiences. Billboards on highways. . . ."

Still an emerging New York State conservation leader, Paul himself led Zahnie into most of these places. He taught the new executive secretary of The Wilderness Society how to stump to save the wilderness, how to build a ground swell at the grass roots.

A few years before Paul died, he captioned a blow-up of the snapshot I made of my father in the late 1950s. The setting is the back yard of our home in the Washington, D.C. suburb of Hyattsville, Maryland. In the snapshot, my father wears a full-brimmed hat and overcoat over a suit with white dress shirt and tie. He carries his small travel suitcase and clutches a portfolio under his free arm. The snapshot ran on the poster to promote the *American Experience* TV series film "Wild by Law," which focuses on Robert Marshall, Aldo Leopold, and Zahnie.

Above and below the photograph Paul has had typed in: "Howard Zahniser: from Washington . . . to New York City, to Albany, to Schenectady, to Buffalo, back to Schenectady, to Watertown, and to Albany again." Those were hearings and meetings Paul and Zahnie did together during the Black River War. I went with my father by train when he attended one of the Buffalo meetings. At five years old, I traveled free. I stayed at a cousin's home while my father did his conservation business.

My father's letter to Paul about the trip closes with one of many, many return solicitations from Zahnie to Paul: "I forgot to ask you when you are coming to Washington, but I do wish that you would work it in this winter. You could do a lot of good down here."

Paul could have, for sure. But it would be twelve years before Paul Schaefer did repay all those Black River War debts and testify on Capitol Hill in Washington, D.C. in favor of my father's all-consuming project of federal wilderness legislation.

"It seems incredible that even with all this help, we were able to pull back from the brink of disaster that marvelous Moose River country," Paul concludes his piece for the Friends of the Forest Preserve brochure. "We have been on the defensive too long. It is time to gather our forces and to accomplish things that heretofore have been but dreams."

Paul wrote that in 1955. That same year Zahnie, on behalf of a new national coalition of conservationists, negotiated the final settlement that kept the proposed Echo Park dam—or any other subsequently—from violating the protected lands of Dinosaur National Monument on the Green River in distant Utah. In so many words, and this also in 1955, Zahnie was to exhort a convention in Washington, D.C., with the same theme: It is time to gather our forces and to accomplish things that heretofore have been but dreams: a National Wilderness Preservation System.

Photos: *Above, Howard Zahniser at his cabin in Johnsburg with Crane Mountain in the distance (Ed Zahniser photo); Middle, part of the Moose River Plains saved during the Black River War (John Warren photo).*

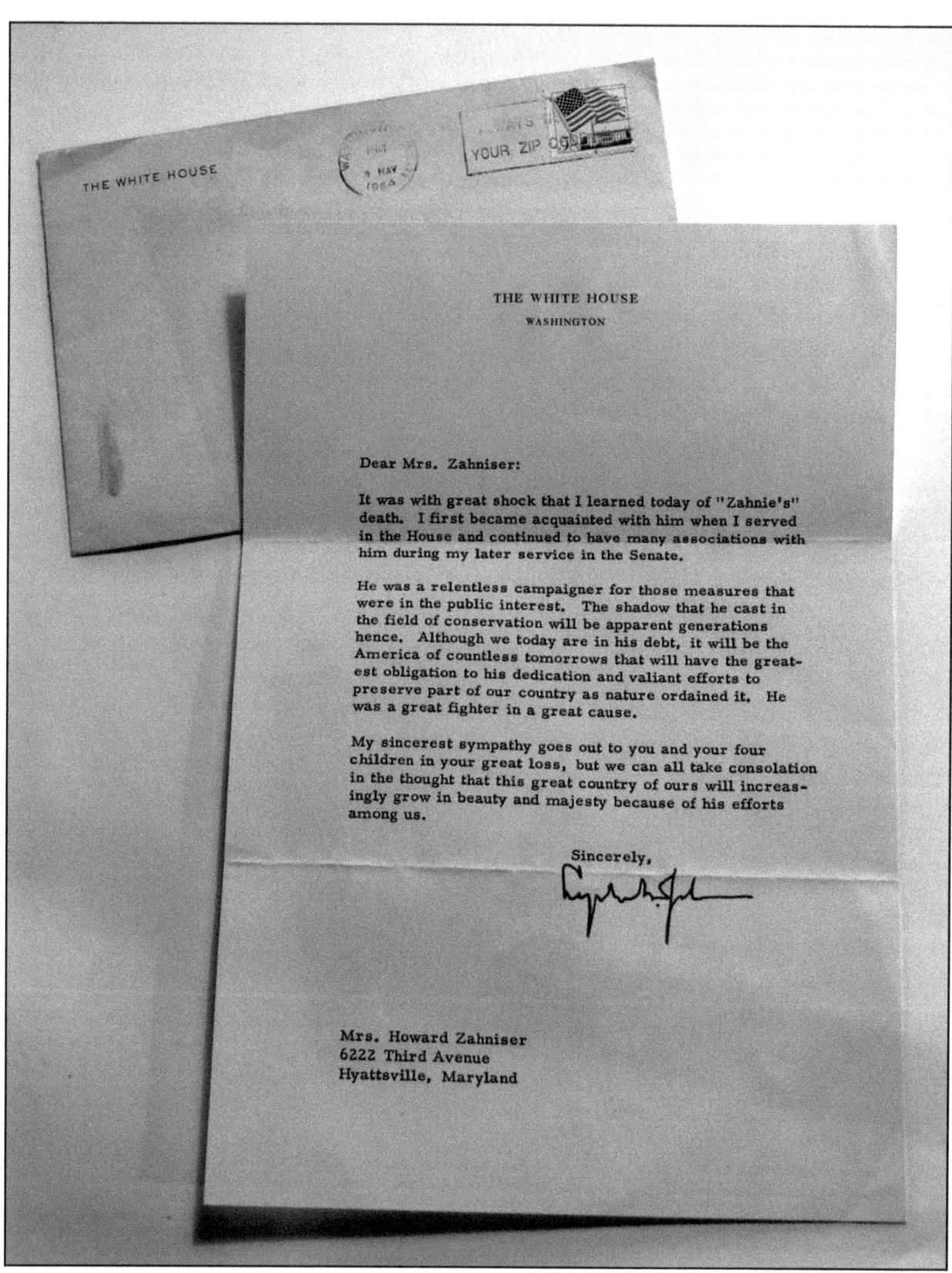

Letter from President Lyndon B. Johnson on the death of Howard Zahniser in 1964.

The Waters of Wildness

"In whatever religious complex we find them, the waters invariably retain their function; they disintegrate, abolish forms, wash away sins; they are at once purifying and regenerating."
—*Mircea Eliade*

It is fitting and proper that people should stare at Adirondack waters in wonder. It was for these waters that the forests, and therefore the land itself, were saved for the posterity you and I and our progeny now are. Verplanck Colvin set this forest wilderness preservation in motion in the 1870s expressly to save the headwaters of much of New York City's water supply and the source and supply of water crucial to the Erie Canal. After enumerating problems of forest destruction in his 1870 account of the "Ascent of Mount Seward," Colvin wrote: "The remedy for this is the creation of an ADIRONDACK PARK or timber preserve, under charge of a forest warden and deputies . . . . The interests of commerce and navigation demand that these forests should be preserved; and for posterity should be set aside, this Adirondack region, as a park for New York, as is the Yosemite for California and the Pacific States.

    The Hudson River flows to sea at New York City but begins its life on a shoulder of Mount Marcy in a small lake first reported by Colvin. He gave it the poetic name Lake Tear of the Clouds. For most of his teenage and adult life, Colvin was a passionate, single-minded advocate of preserving the great Adirondack Mountains forests. In Colvin's time, such people we now know as conservationists and certainly not professional conservationists did not exist. Nor would there be professional environmentalists for another hundred years. Colvin made his passion pay for itself, some of the time, by being a surveyor. His parents fully intended that Colvin should be a lawyer but no dice. All Colvin wanted to do was survey the Adirondacks. John Mitchell has written about Colvin as "The Man Who Married the Mountains."

    Fortunately for those of us attached to the wildlands and wilderness of today's Adirondacks, in the 1870s the New York State legislature did appropriate the money for a surveyor to do what Colvin had lobbied to bring about.

    It is not possible over most of the United States today even to imagine the scale of outright forest destruction that swept across not just New York State but the United States. First came the clearcutting of forests in charcoal-making for the iron industry and then on the timber industry's rapacious sweep across the continent in the second half of the 19th Century. Railroads, which emerged in the late 1820s and 1830s, soon made it possible to log even more extensively. Railroads liberated logging from its necessary marriage to streams and rivers as public highways to float the logs to lumber mills. Belching ash and cinders without spark arresters, locomotives also set the woods and leftover logging slash on fire to a remarkable degree. Denudation and its fiery aftermaths brought devastating flooding in their wake. They threatened to destroy watersheds' ability to retain water for timely delivery to rapidly expanding populations downstream.

The Erie and other canals reached their heydays in the 1850s through the 1870s. Their owners and operators grew gravely concerned about the forest destruction that often featured their fiercest, upstart transportation competitor, the railroad. Lack of healthy forests would disrupt crucial supplies of the water without which their thirsty ditches would be forced to shut down operations.

Today, we little remember the extent to which the opening of the Erie Canal created New York City as world trade center and major metropolis. Pre-canal Gotham was dwarfed by East Coast port cities Boston, Philadelphia, and Baltimore. No mental stretch is required, however, to visualize the extent to which the Hudson River—with headwaters in the Adirondacks—delivers water to the the metropolis the Erie Canal enabled. Indeed, its waters mostly supply the more than 60 percent water content of each voter in one of the nation's most concentrated blocks of voters.

Colvin, a native of New York State's capital city of Albany, understood and acted on these facts. Out west in California's Sierra Nevada Colvin's contemporary John Muir was similarly observing that mountain forests were fountains of water and therefore fountains of life.

Colvin measured the Adirondack Mountains from 1872 into the 1890s with a scientific vengeance fueled by the desire to see their forest fountain watersheds conserved if not preserved. It all came down to water by way of trees as forests: the history of the conservation movement in the United States is the story of Americans and our forests. The Adirondacks tell the whole story in microcosm, from protected parks and forests to designated wilderness and wild rivers. Evelyn Greene, Paul Schaefer's daughter, is an Adirondack 46'er from her youth and a board member of both the Residents Committee to Protect the Adirondacks and the Association for the Protection of the Adirondacks. When she stares at the Hudson River rapids from the highway bridge at the Glen in winter or on its banks at the Ice Meadows, Evelyn knows this conservation story in her bones.

Left: Paul Schaefer, ca. 1950. Photographer unknown. *Right*: John Apperson and Paul Schaefer, ca. 1946, Photo by Howard Zahniser.

Paul Schaefer with John Apperson, ca. 1947, the only known photo of the two together, taken by Howard Zahniser (Adirondack Research Library of Protect the Adirondacks). See more at: https://www.adirondackalmanack.com/2014/08/wilderness-50th-howard-zahniser-and-the-black-river-war.html

Paul Schaefer on the porch of his Beaver House cabin just off the extension of Edwards Hill Road, 600 feet below the Zahniser's Mateskared Cabin. Photo by Ken Rimany.

Paul Schaefer: The Glue for New York State Wilderness

*[Religious persons] refuse to live solely in what, in modern
terms, is called the historical present; they attempt to regain a sacred time
that, from one point of view, can be homologized to eternity."*
—*Mircea Eliade*

My first childhood memories of Paul Schaefer are of his hands. They seemed huge to me, big enough to serve as lasts for making baseball gloves. I also remember Paul from my earliest Adirondack summers as a quality of expectancy.

On early 1950s Wednesday nights, we four Zahniser kids used to sit on the big wood beam Paul had placed in front of our outdoor fireplace at Mateskared and wait for his pickup truck headlights to turn off Route 8 onto Edwards Hill Road. In those days you could still see the hamlet, Bakers Mills from our cabin side yard.

Headlights on Route 8 at Bakers Mills two miles south of Mateskared. Headlights heading up Edwards Hill Road generated immediate tension. Would they make it as far as the second bridge—about half of the two miles from Route 8 to Mateskared—without turning off into a driveway?

"Do you think that's Paul?" we kids would ask each other. Or if we were feeling expansive, "I bet that's Paul's truck."

Paul came to the Adirondacks from his home in Schenectady on Wednesday nights and again on Saturday afternoons or evenings. He'd drive back to Schenectady in time for work on Thursday and Monday mornings. There was no high-speed Adirondack Northway then—but Paul was well known for his heavy foot on the gas pedal.

As I grew older, Paul's out-sized character did not diminish but shifted and, for me, expressed itself in less physical ways. When Paul worked in a group of diverse hunters and anglers and other conservationists, his outsized character showed as part innocence and part egolessness. Time and again, Paul helped such groups find a common conservation stance—especially to defend wilderness and the Forest Preserve—even though many in the gathering might have seen the issue as tangential to their core commitments or interests.

Indeed, there is remarkable raw video footage of Paul accepting a conservation award. Right before your eyes Paul turns the event into a celebration not of himself but of the organization giving him the award. A focus group would no doubt remember Paul as the presenter, not recipient.

Paul retained a lifelong innocence of character most of us probably lose by our mid-teens. This innocence was buttressed by his winning grin. No doubt Paul's own felt lack of formal education—he left school at age 15 to help support the family—lay behind his seeming self-effacement. Paul was a life-long learner who admired scholars, scientists, and other writers. He educated himself continually by digesting the best of their works. But this sense of personal lack no doubt helped stoke his desire to build a major personal library around the Adirondacks that he had begun to love even before he had to leave formal schooling behind.

Fortunately, very early in his budding love affair with these mountains, Paul read Verplanck Colvin, who had led the massive survey of the Adirondacks in the late 1800s. As Paul later wrote, "Colvin's writing made me want to learn as much as possible about the Adirondacks and why he would write such beautiful prose for submission to state agencies."

Paul's admiration for Colvin as a writer later extended to my father Howard Zahniser, known as Zahnie, in this curious regard—the ability and determination to write beautiful prose for other than literary purposes. Paul's admiration for the goals of the Wilderness Act was matched by his admiration for the poetic prose of its Section 2. That section includes the statement of purpose and definition of wilderness my father largely crafted and polished:

Sec. 2. (a) In order to assure that an increasing population, accompanied by expanding settlement and growing mechanization, does not occupy and modify all areas within the United States and its possessions, leaving no lands designated for preservation and protection in their natural condition, it is hereby declared to be the policy of the Congress to secure for the American people of present and future generations the benefits of an enduring resource of wilderness. . . . (c) A wilderness, in contrast with those areas where man and his own works dominate the landscape, is hereby recognized as an area where the earth and its community of life are untrammeled by man, where man himself is a visitor who does not remain.

That careful prose of Section 2(c) now also defines the designated wilderness on New York State Forest Preserve lands. No one knew more intimately than Paul Schaefer that this was no coincidence. Paul amassed an archive to prove the point.

Paul represented a positive conservation anachronism as he dogged the sportsmen-preservationist alliance that he kept alive by the strength of his own personality as both hunter-angler and ardent conservationist. No question, Paul was the longtime glue for New York State's wilderness movement, the glue that conservationist David Brower, in the late 1990s, lamented was lacking for the contemporary national wilderness movement.

Paul brought forward the formative sportsmen-backed 1870s' conservation thrust of Theodore Roosevelt and the Boone and Crockett Club. Mainly through his personality, he helped ally that thrust with post-Earth Day 1970s environmental politics. Paul eventually became New York State's elder statesman hunter-conservationist. No doubt his intimacy with Verplanck Colvin's writings helped Paul embody this bridge between old-school sportsmen-conservationists and post-Earth Day environmentalists.

"Howard Zahniser and I had a very fine relationship on matters Adirondack from the time that he acquired his cabin in the Adirondacks to his death in 1964," Paul wrote in the early 1990s. "We climbed mountains, walked wilderness trails, attended hearings of State Legislative Committees, public hearings of River Regulating Boards, and conventions of the New York State Conservation Council in many parts of the State. In addition to these rather frequent get-togethers at his cabin or mine in the Adirondacks, we met numerous times with members of the [New York State] Conservation Council both here in the Adirondack Room at St. David's Lane and elsewhere in the State. By happy coincidence, in our discussions it seemed that Howard's philosophy of wilderness and the way to preserve it was substantially identical to mine."

My father paid periodic homage to Paul's stature as a conservationist. Typical is this short letter Zahnie wrote to Paul on Wilderness Society letterhead in November 1955, just *before* a decisive state vote on the continuing sanctity of the Forest Preserve: *"Dear Paul: This may reach you on the eve of the election next Tuesday and, if so, it will I hope carry with it an expression of deep appreciation for the wonderful way in which you have carried the large campaign against amendment No. 7. Win or lose, we owe you another great debt of gratitude."*

As he so often did, Zahnie closed his epistle with an appeal for Paul to come to Washington, D.C., to help stir up interest in the national wilderness legislation that my father would draft two months later.

I know of Paul Schaefer's leaving New York State only two times, in both cases to come to Washington, once with the family on a largely social holiday visit and then again to testify at a hearing on the wilderness bill in 1962. "Wilderness is not a luxury," Paul told the members of Congress at that hearing, "it is a dire necessity in this age and will become even more precious as the years go on."

How well Paul knew that—as a next-door neighbor to what is now the New York State Siamese Ponds Wilderness Area. And I think he knows it still. Paul Schaefer had a significant impact on the national wilderness preservation scene despite how few times he left New York.

Paul Schaefer's Adirondack epicenter definitely sat on Edwards Hill Road in what he called "cabin country." This was where his family first came for summers to help his mother escape airborne allergies when Paul was still a boy. This was where Paul had moved a 100-year-old cabin onto land next to his family of origin's cabin land near Edwards Hill Road off Route 8 out of Bakers Mills, N.Y. This was where in his youth local neighbors tutored him in Adirondack ways—and where as an adult he would roundly shock them by *planting* trees, which they told him "were for cutting, not for planting." This was where, in the early 1960s he built his Beaver House so his hunting party, the Cataract Club, would have a place to gather, as would the many meetings of New York state conservationists he subsequently convened there.

In the mid-1960s, Paul built the first of two cabins over on the Chatiemac Road, east of Edwards Hill Road off Route 8. Soon he began staying over there more than at the Beaver House right down our hill and across our mutual unpaved, final stretch of Edwards Hill Road. It worried me that he might be forsaking his roots here.

"You won't lose interest in Edwards Hill and sell your land over here, will you?" I asked him one day. We sat on our porch at Mateskared. Paul sat closest to the road and to his land on the other side of it. Seated between me and Eleventh Mountain, Paul seemed momentarily lost in looking toward it for a spell.

Mine had been a direct, personal question. It had taken me a long time to work up the nerve to pose it to him. These weren't the days of men's sensitivity groups, and fathers often qualified as our most distant relatives.

Paul's first reaction was to look back over at Eleventh Mountain, not at me. When he did speak moments later, it was straightforward, looking down the valley, almost as though addressing not me so much as Crane Mountain due south of us.

"Of course not," Paul said. "This place means the world to me."

The Whole Scheme of Life

"... periodic return to the sacred time of origin" is not "a rejection of the real world and an escape into dream and imagination.... It is at once a thirst for the sacred and nostalgia for being."
—Mircea Eliade

Howard Zahniser wrote the following in his monthly *Nature Magazine* book review column in 1945, the year before he met Paul Schaefer and first came to the Adirondacks. Nevertheless, Paul would have been one of the "few of those" my father invokes in his book review:

"Many of us seldom get, or take, the opportunity to sense the magnitude of the whole scheme of Life of which we are only a part. We know only the rush of human events, and we seldom even challenge the presumption of those who call this rush the march of time. Only a few of those who are in the midst of this rush, and it includes us all, can ever be expected to break pace long enough to fall in step with the greater procession that moves through the natural seasons."

By 1935, despite his evangelical Christian upbringing, my father had already suggested that "Nature's celebrations ... are inexhaustible sources of interest and delight and revelation." This reflected the mid-1800s idea—articulated by Emerson, Thoreau, and others—that Nature is God's Second Book. In 1938, Zahnie wrote that Nature was "something conducive to, if not an object of, worship." Note the hedging phrase: "if not an object of..." Both Zahnie and his Adirondack wilderness mentor Paul Schaefer held essentially religious views of life. The word *religious* shares roots with *ligament* and, for typography mavens, *ligature*. Religion means what binds us to the cosmos, whose Greek form *kosmos*, as Thoreau writes in his essay "Walking," means not only world but beauty, pattern, and order.

Paul was Catholic by faith via his family of origin. Two things for which I caught hell from Paul over the two summers that I worked for him were both sins of omission, not commission. The first happened while we were staying at his Beaver House on Edwards Hill Road one weekend. One Sunday morning I let him sleep too late to make mass at either Wevertown or North Creek. No matter that I knew he was exhausted and needed to catch up on his sleep.

Paul was in earnest about attending mass, but that was not the end of his religious practice. Noel Reidinger-Johnson, biographer of Jeanne Robert Foster, worked with Paul on a number of conservation film and writing projects. She writes that:

"Religion for Paul was a way of life, not a Sunday happening. Paul's large, angular frame walked to the rhythm of a higher call, one that demanded he submerge his ego, forego materialism, and use his mind and talents for the betterment of humankind and not the self. This was his outsizedness. He would hand a copy of St. Francis's prayer to people, for this was the creed by which he lived, one he hoped others could adopt. *Lord, make me an instrument of Thy peace. . .* He brought together warring factions. He included rather than excluded . . . *where there is hatred let me sow love . . .* He extended himself and whatever he had to others . . . *where there is injury, pardon . . .* He held no grudge for those who took advantage of his generosity or weakness."

The other time I caught hell from Paul showed that his work ethic could have as readily sprung from Calvinist theology as from Roman Catholic theology. This happened one Schenectady weekday morning. Again, I knew Paul was whipped and had gotten to bed very late the night before. So I let him sleep-in when he evidently hadn't meant to. When he woke up and realized we were already a half-hour late for work, he was fit to be tied.

In reality, I awakened Paul at the St. David's Lane homestead but once or twice in my two summers there. Paul got up on his own. I should have been surprised on this explosive occasion that it was now *my fault* that he overslept.

To put it mildly, Paul was given to impatience, particularly if what was at issue was life in general and not conservation politics in particular. In my experience of Paul, this came out most markedly when we would be driving from the house on St. David's Lane to one of multiple construction job sites he routinely ran. Usually Paul dropped me off to play go-fer for the carpenters, plasterers, or mason. Sometimes I got to play laborer for his brother-in-law foreman "Uncle" Nat Keseburg, Paul's wife Carolyn's brother, a wonderfully genuine character.

Stopped at a red light in his pickup truck in downtown Schenectady, Paul would get impatient with the delay and nervously tap lightly and rhythmically on the horn. This had nothing to do with the drivers in front of us, but it sometimes had a marked effect on them. Paul seemed genuinely startled by resulting driver outbursts—as though his horn tapping was less than conscious. When required by his quest to preserve Adirondack wilderness, Paul possessed uncanny patience and equanimity, enough for himself and others. Dave Gibson of Adirondack Wild, Friends of the Forest Preserve, spoke to this quality of Paul's conservation personality at the time of Paul's death.

"In the early 1990s, Paul and I drove . . . from a meeting in Warrrensburg," Gibson reminisced. "I was discouraged by the apparently bitter turn of events and emotions since the unveiling of the report from the Commission on the Adirondacks a year earlier. Paul told me not to be. He said 'the Commission report will surely accelerate events, just as the building of this Northway forced the creation of the Adirondack Park Agency because of the human presence and pressure that this road induced.' Paul did not fear acceleration of events, nor controversy, because he carried with him an unquenchable belief that if persons had the right attitude and an enthusiasm commensurate with the history and potential greatness of the Adirondacks, then the acceleration and the controversy would be colored and flavored and directed with devotion and respect and care."

Paul's lack of "fear acceleration of events" is perhaps well expressed by Noel Reidinger-Johnson: "Paul's spiritual perspective yielded enormous consequences for the conservation movement. His voice became one that people trusted, one that attracted diversified groups of people to form the coalition that in turn gave Nature a voice in the New York legislature. In his writing and photography, Paul transformed abstract values into concrete reality." Paul's ability to communicate hope, Noel says, "hope that there was a future, a timeless future for man," could move listeners to tears. "Paul personified the fact that man was but a small part of a greater whole, governed by a universal force far greater than the self. He taught that 'dominion over the fish of the sea and over the birds of the air and over every living thing that moves upon the earth' meant stewardship of natural resources for the countless generations that would inherit the earth."

For Paul stewardship included commitment to preserving wilderness, according to Reidinger-Johnson: "This meant that wilderness had to be set aside in order that people could step outside the rush of the everyday to reconnect with God. This was Paul's life work. He summed it up in the final paragraph of *Adirondack Cabin Country*:

> "I can go inside now, confident that the youth in the distant tomorrow's will backpack down winding forest trails, glimpse the silver of a wilderness lake shining through the trees, and gather around their crackling campfire. They, too, will experience the freedom of spirit and the indescribable happiness found in solitude, enriched by the song of the hermit thrush, the hoot of an owl, or the cry of a loon. They will talk about a climb to a storm-swept mountain summit or a trip down the canyon of a wild river. And before taking to their sleeping bags under starlit heavens, they will talk about how they can make possible similar experiences for the legions of youth who will hunger for adventures as they have. I can go inside knowing that an ancient log cabin, the Beaver House, and *Adirondack Cabin Country* have played a part in crystallizing this priceless heritage."

Zahnie shared such spiritual grounding and likewise drew a kind of 'sustenance for the struggle' from Mateskared's character as a neighbor to the wilderness and wildness that are still "the potential greatness of the Adirondacks." Zahnie's "place" was in this sense smaller than Paul Schaefer's sense of place here. Paul's reached out to the larger whole that expressed itself as the Adirondacks or an even less delimited North Country. The Adirondacks have a Blue Line around them. The North Country reaches beyond that line. Where to, I was never sure. But Paul's Adirondack epicenter sat here on Edwards Hill in his "cabin country."

Howard Zahniser's Culture Heroes

"A howling wilderness seldom ever howls.
The howling is chiefly done by the imagination of the traveler."
—Henry David Thoreau

Howard Zahniser's important role in mid-1900s wildlands conservation, both nationally and in the Adirondacks, was culturally grounded in the works of three poets and a book in the Hebrew Scriptures: Dante Alighieri, William Blake, and Henry David Thoreau, and "The Book of Job." Thoreau is not widely known as a poet today, but that's how he embarked on his initially rocky literary career, which time eventually made secure. As the late Thoreau scholar Robert D. Richardson writes, "The two years Thoreau spent at Walden Pond and the night he spent in the Concord jail are among the most familiar features of the American intellectual landscape."

Thoreau's mentor and sometime employer Ralph Waldo Emerson had bought—for a woodlot—the Walden Pond property on which Thoreau squatted for two years. Emerson had also first sallied forth as Poet, with a capital P—or even capital OP, for Orphic Poet. Emerson early pictured the career of the poet as like the role of Orpheus in Greek myth. Orpheus descends into the Underworld to re-emerge as the Bearer of Truth. Emerson's Poet was projected to stand at the core of society and speak forth oracles to give the world direction. It's difficult, if not impossible, to imagine such a poet's role today.

The timing wasn't that great even back then. Emerson was contemporaneous with Swiss biologist, geologist, and scholar of Earth's natural history, Louis Agassiz, PhD and MD. Emerson was to champion Agassiz's views in America. But Emerson championed Agassiz not in Emerson's role as Poet, a role he early abandoned, but as a former preacher turned popular lecturer, eminent essayist, and philosopher.

Poetry proved to be at the utmost, trailing end of its influence as a venue for public discourse then. Our family's Adirondack cabin, Mateskared, similarly had been at the trailing end of Adirondack subsistence agriculture and was destined to become a neighbor to wilderness. Modernist poet Ezra Pound—born late in Emerson's 1800s—completed university studies in the early 1900s. By then, American poetry had been reduced to the status of the lyric. Pound could not imagine the absurdity of an adult male career in America devoted to the lyric poem. He expatriated to Europe not long after graduating from the University of Pennsylvania in 1905.

Poetry was then already headed full-tilt away from society's core toward the peripheries. A. R. Ammons taught poetry writing at Cornell University starting in

1964. Born the son of North Carolina sharecroppers, he would hold the Goldwin Smith Chair in Poetry at Cornell until retiring in 1998. Among his contemporary poets, Ammons probably most inherited the Emersonian tradition of poetic concerns. He titled one of his book-length poems *Garbage*. He locates this indicator phenomenon (an actual landfill he saw stand like a ziggurat along Interstate 95) at the urban edge of our inanely consumptive society:

> *. . . if I reap the peripheries will I*
> *get hardened seed and dried roughage, roughage*
> *like teasel and cattail and brush above snow in*
> *winter, pure design lifeless in a painted hold.*

Henry Thoreau expatriated from poetry to prose and pictured Walden Pond—which lay at booming intellectual Concord's periphery—as his oracle. Thoreau only figured out the career thing quite late in his comparatively short life. Eventually, he seems to have decided his career constituted the keeping of his journal. For a writer, Thoreau's was a fantastically devoted commitment, the taking of a solitary vow that has long haunted me. Today, however, Thoreau's journals are key players in climate change studies in New England via phenology, the study of changes in the first annual plant bloomings and animal migrations. Thoreau observed and reported them faithfully for years.

Dante, Blake, and Thoreau: my father's triumvirate of heroes is more consistent than first glance might suggest. Dante's *Comedy*—only later was the mis-label "Divine" set to this great poem, supposing it religious allegory—has a wilderness subtheme. As Nicholas Kilmer and some other scholars read it, Dante's poem has a markedly political drive as well.

Dante broke with literary and cultural tradition by adopting what he saw as vernacular Italian as his language of poetry. He also sets up a concept of the forest edge as a boundary between civilization and wildness. Blake prophetically railed against the heretical idolatry of elevating rationalism as a metaphysic. Thoreau fenced with human social foibles, trying to ferret out how wildness is somehow a tonic that promises no less than preservation of the world.

Dante, Blake, and Thoreau pioneer contemporary edge effects that time and literary tradition will, like madly whirling centripetal forces, reposition close to the axis or core of our cultural consciousness.

"I am beginning to realize that poetry was a big part of who your father was," Zahnie's biographer Mark Harvey told me. He had just read, in the library at Pennsylvania State University, my father's late 1930s and early 1940s "Nature in Print" book review columns in *Nature Magazine*.

My father read a great deal of poetry. He also wrote poetry occasionally, some of which was published under the pen name Archibald Howard, combining his father's and his own first names. *The Scientific Monthly* published his long poem "America Grows Corn," which was based on actual statistics of corn varieties and corn production in the United States. However, beginning in fall 1945, Zahnie's career became centered on wilderness preservation.

Mateskared became a touchstone for his career interest. Indeed, the Adirondack Black River Wars occasioned his introduction to the region. With Paul Schaefer, he traveled the western Adirondacks building opposition, both popular and political, to a series of dams projected for building on and flooding "forever wild" Forest Preserve lands. In the end, the dams were not to be built.

During summer vacations at Mateskared, Zahnie worked on several of the 66 drafts through which, over eight years, he shepherded the wording of the federal wilderness legislation, beginning in early 1956. Five months after his death in May 1964, the Wilderness Act established the National Wilderness Preservation System. The Act now protects 111 million acres of federal public lands in their wild state.

At his Mateskared writing table, Zahnie could lean back and look out the double-hung cabin window at distant Crane Mountain. Who knows what thoughts its isolated granitic monolith inspired? Might one or two reside in that wilderness statute protecting "an enduring resource of wilderness?" The Wilderness Act called into question—revised, even—the very notion of the Myth of Progress against which William Blake and Henry Thoreau had railed.

Mateskared Cabin.

'There Is A Wolf in Me!'

My late sister Esther Gillies was a therapist in London, England. She specialized in voice dialogue therapy. This therapy attempts to engage the client's heretofore unacknowledged multiple inner voices in constructive dialogue with each other. Esther was highly intuitive. As an adult, she could still work up her own fright by recalling from childhood our father reciting a poem that she and I remembered as "There Is a Wolf in Me," by Carl Sandburg (1878–1967). As it turns out, the poem is titled "Wilderness:"

> *There is a wolf in me . . . fangs pointed for tearing gashes . . .*
> *a red tongue for raw meat . . . and the hot lapping of blood—*
> *I keep this wolf because the wilderness gave it to me*
> *and the wilderness will not let it go.*

I can still conjure my father reciting the poem to us as he stood framed by the doorway from our kitchen pantry-way into the dining room of our childhood home in the Hyattsville, Maryland suburb of Washington, D.C.

No matter that the house no longer exists. No matter that our father Howard Zahniser died in 1964, when I was a freshman in college. No matter that I have since seen wolves in the wild and witnessed their extreme wariness toward their bipedal primate nemesis humankind.

What was so frightening about the poem may be the fact that, truth to tell, there is probably a wolf in each of us. What if *my* wolf got out? What if *your* wolf got out?

What was so frightening about the poem may have been that our household operated under a multi-generation taboo on anger. The taboo in our religious family system invalidated strong emotion. Yet this poem poured forth with dramatic force from the alpha-male enforcer of that taboo, the one who sometimes reacted angrily to our child-like shows of anger. What made the poem so frightening was our undoubted anxiety: Who or what might we kill or maim if we were ever to let ourselves feel the full force of our own anger?

There Is a Wolf in Me: Was our suburban veneer of civilization so thin as the poem's perceived force implied?

What may have been so frightening was how the poem connected my father to a forceful inner freedom that his normal parental role prevented his children's seeing. What if our meal ticket and half our parental all-purpose security blanket should revert to the wild?

I once broached with my late sister Karen our father's reciting this poem. "I *hated* that poem!" she said. I now understand the poem's startling force in our childhood as wildness welling up from within our human condition.

Around our family cabin Mateskared and throughout the Adirondacks, wolves were long since extirpated, made regionally extinct, so to speak. Now Mateskared and not the wolf stands as a boundary figure on this margin or ecotone between civilization and the wilderness. No houses dot the hill above us now, but only two or three cellar dents revealing where a small house or a shack once stood.

No doubt the wolf found berths in our psyches through the great forests cloaking northern Europe after the late great Ice Ages withdrew. As Robert Pogue Harrison writes, all we of European stock carry still that deep forest image in our consciousness. Europe's wolf lived in those thick, post-Ice Age blanketings of forest. The final act of war in Europe used to be to kill off the wolves that had multiplied along with wartime human body counts. Like many arch predators, wolves are also opportunistic scavengers.

Those great wolf-inhabited forests were that wilderness out of which, as Aldo Leopold declares in *A Sand County Almanac*, the artifact of our civilization has been derived—*hammered* was the verb Leopold settled on. Leopold borrowed his metaphorical pre-industrial hammer from Henry David Thoreau. In the "Chesuncook" chapter of *The Maine Woods*, Thoreau hits a similar, albeit hand-cut, nail on the head. Wilderness is "the raw material of all our civilization" and not just in the commodity sense but in a larger sense as well. Thoreau described himself as a "border figure" between civilization and the wildness that preoccupies not only his essay "Walking" but also chunks of *Walden*, *The Maine Woods*, and *Cape Cod*.

On Thoreau's *Cape Cod*, shore, coast, and beach are, like Mateskared, ecotones, edge phenomena, a wild and strange borderland between *terra firma* and the vast wilderness of the sea.

The wild was Thoreau's holy land, Robert D. Richardson Jr. wrote.

". . . Thoreau came to practice a kind of 'wilding therapy,'" Lawrence Buell maintains, "as a method for keeping himself as defamiliarized as possible during what might otherwise have become boringly routine activities. . . ."

Defamiliarized: Thoreau could imagine a small brook as the Orinoco or Mississippi rivers. He would walk alone at night in order to feel what it was like to be the first or the last human.

Defamiliarized: The late great Adirondack conservationist Paul Schaefer 'discovered' Nate Davis Pond, which the State of New York didn't know it owned. I am projecting here, but not, I think, by much: Paul imagined himself at the side of his hero Verplanck Colvin's on Marcy's flank at Lake Tear of the Clouds, the

Hudson headwaters. His was the same quest Bob Marshall took up in subarctic Alaska: the quest for 'the world as it was.'

Defamiliarized: Mateskared rests in a shrinking ecotone. Mateskared is a closing edge between civilization and the wilderness.

I am told one comes to terms with a living parent more readily than with a dead parent. Our old tapes prove our eternal aspect. Attics and safety deposit boxes hoard only the ephemeral by contrast. Siblings become therapists and pastoral counselors too late to do us the most good. *That* would be while we yet lived the very childhoods that provide us, as Flannery O'Connor asserted, enough material to work on for the rest of our lives.

My sister Karen recalled a curious anecdote of our early teen years. Perhaps her own priestly duties as an adult swinging the censer or thurible awakened for her this anecdotal memory—of Roman Catholic Father Bruno in our childhood suburban living room speaking strange litanies in Latin, even more strange to us as teenaged Protestants. If there were a wolf in my father, what might he have suspected in our household that moved him to invite the young Catholic seminarian to bless (or exorcise?) our home. My evangelical grandparents would have rolled over in their four graves like synchronized swimmers at the mere thought of Roman Catholic ritual invading their hopes for our "good Christian home." We were Presbyterians by then.

Father Bruno was the friend of a family friend. He stood at least six feet tall, darkly northern Mediterranean in looks, as I recall him. In his complementary dark, priestly street garb, Father Bruno struck my child self as taller yet, mythic even, large-screen like the scene in the movie "Black Robe" as the protagonist plunges ahead into the winter wilderness. Father Bruno was studying at his order's seminary attached to The Catholic University of America. The university lay on my father's commuting route from our Maryland suburb to his office at The Wilderness Society, located then on P Street NW, just off Dupont Circle in downtown Washington, D.C.

The ritual was foreign enough to seem, in the usualness of our late-1950s living room, like stepping inside the black-and-white television my father would not admit into that family space. Could Father Bruno's ritual be where Karen got the primal impetus to her priestly vocation she took up in mid-life? Even opera sounds important in a strange tongue. Father Bruno sprinkled water about our living room.

Father Bruno's blessing didn't save our childhood house from the road. This was symbolic retribution perhaps—posthumous payback for how hard our father, as primary author of and chief lobbyist for the National Wilderness Preservation System, fought to keep roads out of remnant wilderness areas. That was the big threat to big wilderness then: the roads for automobiles penetrating it, carving it up. The automobile had invented suburbia.

The automobile threatened to push suburbia into the whole of the country, into wildness and wilderness, too. Seventy five percent of "We the people" now lives in this suburbia the car invented. The National Wilderness Preservation System now protects just more than 111 million acres of federal public lands. It also provided the definition for New York State's wilderness system, whose Siamese Ponds Wilderness Area now borders Mateskared. All forms of mechanized travel are largely excluded from federal wilderness except in Alaska. But even 109 million acres make nowhere near a tithe of our landscapes here in North America, on Turtle Island.

Or maybe *only* Father Bruno's blessing kept our house standing while my father still lived. When the house did come down, we had already buried my father along the Allegheny River in Tionesta, Pennsylvania, his childhood home whose Indian name means "home of the wolves." Since our suburban house came down, Mateskared has become the gathering place for our increasingly far-flung family. For me, it became a space of centering down, like a dog circles his or her tail before plopping down to nap.

Ducks on Carps' Backs, Walking

People say everyday mind isn't our Buddha nature.
I say our Buddha nature is everyday mind.
—Stonehouse

On rainy nights, if you listen closely, you can hear opera music coming out of the stout wooden bench in front of our Adirondack cabin's fieldstone fireplace. That's what Paul Schaefer told us when he brought us the piece of beam and said it would make a fine bench for our indoor fireplace. Paul owned a contracting business in Schenectady, New York, building early-American style homes. Paul and my father Howard Zahniser were also Adirondack conservation partners, beginning in 1946, when I was six months old. Paul had served as middle-man when my parents, who lived in a Maryland suburb of Washington, D.C., bought our cabin from Harold and Pansy Allen later that August. Pansy owned the farm adjacent to and downhill from Mateskared.

Paul claimed to have salvaged the large, hand-hewn beam from the old Albany Opera House. Over the years, he said, the beam soaked up more high culture than it could contain when the relative humidity rises indoors.

In truth, as I only learned decades later, the beam came from the stone chapel on Chapel Street near Albany's Ten Eyck Hotel. It was a roof beam in a large, open room that officers of the American Revolution frequented for dances. Paul had used a piece of the same timber in the Adirondack room of his stone home in Schenectady, now part of the Union College Kelly Adirondack Center.

We Americans have expected much from our forests and their trees and wood, but even a centuries-seasoned, hand-hewn timber of such proportions —however long supportive of the arts—could be expected to retain only so many operatic arias indefinitely.

When Paul brought us the bench beam, our cabin, Mateskared, had no electricity. Zahnie frowned on vacation radio use. He agreed with ecologist Aldo Leopold that the best outdoor recreation was that which stood in sharpest contrast to one's work-a-day life. Nevertheless, music wafting into cabin life on a rainy night from our fireplace bench would not have been unwelcome. My mother Alice was a trained coloratura soprano.

Zahnie was a great joke teller, but when it came to the peculiar genre of tall tales, I remember his besting Paul Schaefer but once. He pulled this off by telling Paul a fish story that was absolutely true. It just sounded like it had to be a tall tale.

Both my parents were native Pennsylvanians. Zahnie told Paul that the Keystone State boasted a large reservoir thickly populated with carp overfed by tourists. Just behind its dam, within food-tossing range of tourists, Zahnie said, the carp were so thick that ducks walked about on the carps' backs to scarf up bread intended for the fish.

My father told Paul this tale late one night at Mateskared, no doubt with dramatic flourishes and precise comedic timing. I was five years old and already fast asleep upstairs.

"Nonsense!" was Paul's pronouncement on Zahnie's story. "That's ridiculous."

But my father insisted on his story's truth. My mother backed him up.

"*Nah*, that's ridiculous!" Paul pronounced the word "*ruh* dik' *uh luss*."

"What if we got Edward up, and he told the same story?" my father challenged Paul.

"Nonsense!" my mother pronounced to both of them, not looking forward to reactivating me after having accomplished the chore of getting me off to sleep. It was a task doubly difficult whenever Paul, whom I idolized, was present and holding forth with his outsized Adirondack tales and lore. I thought Paul was what the Adirondacks would be like if they could walk and talk, too.

At length, Paul and my father persuaded my mother to make this great sacrifice for the sake of settling the issue of the ducks walking on carp backs.

When I was sufficiently awake to talk, I proceeded to corroborate, in enthusiastic detail, my father's fish story. At the bread stand, you could even buy stale round loaves of bread. Tourists would fling them as far out into the dam as they could. Because carp have small, suction mouths, all they could do was push the hardened, stale round loaves up and down the reservoir, waiting for them to get soggy enough to eat.

All this was, indeed a true story of our then-recent family trip to the Pymatuning Reservoir in Pennsylvania. The trip's larger mission had been to visit Robert Griggs, a member of the governing council of The Wilderness Society, for whom my father worked since late three months before I was born in 1945.

Dr. Griggs, as we kids knew the retired scientist, lived near the reservoir. He had led the National Geographic Society expeditions to the vast Katmai, Alaska region and its Valley of Ten Thousand Smokes after the massive 1912 volcanic eruption of Novarupta there. No doubt Dr. Griggs could have regaled Paul with true tales taller than the Adirondacks' highest peak.

Paul's response might still have been "Nonsense! That's *ruh* dik' *uh lous*!" The latter pronouncement was more epithet than adjective for Paul, and

Southern Comfort could make it even more pronounced. The way he pronounced it softened the word's impact many later years when it came as criticism for my errant thinking or foolhardy action. I was to work two of my high school summers for Paul in Schenectady.

Before the first moonwalk, I don't recall Paul's ever admitting any superlative existed outside the Adirondacks, Catskills, or New York State. No doubt that partly inspired my father's ploy— setting his tall but true fish tale in my parents' native Pennsylvania next door. Until my father finally persuaded him to come to Washington, D.C. to testify in favor of the national wilderness legislation, I'm not sure Paul Schaefer had ever been outside the Empire State. Still, he held the entire known world as inadequate compared to the Adirondacks and New York State.

Truth to tell, I have never heard, even on the rainiest of cabin nights, our fireplace bench beam breakout in an aria or the cocky banter of Revolutionary War officers. But having once watched ducks scavenge stale bread by walking on the backs of massed swimming carp, I do listen when cabin conditions just might be right.

The Zahniser family in 1946 (minus Edward) and Schaefer family on Cragorehol porch. Photo by Howard Zahniser (delayed release shutter). LEFT TO RIGHT. Front row: Mathias Zahniser, Evelyn Schaefer, Cub Schaefer, Esther Zahniser, Karen Zahniser, Mary Schaefer. Back row: Howard Zahniser, Alice Zahniser, Carolyn Schaefer, Paul Schaefer. Monica Schaefer might have been napping, or hidden behind Esther Zahniser, in Carolyn Schaefer's lap.

Alice Zahniser at 13th Lake in the 1950's

Mateskared: Builders and First Inhabitants

"One of the great gifts of a cabin is the detachment that it makes possible, the creation of a world of your own."
— *Walter Collins O'Kane*

In 1996, Harold Allen reminisced about my father Howard Zahniser and our family cabin now known as Mateskared: *"He bought the place, and he never had seen it,"* Harold said. *"Paul Schaefer was the one who told him about it."*

Pansy Allen and I were seated at their kitchen table. Her parents, John and Hester Dalaba, had named their girls for plants—Pansy, Daisy, Blossom, Fern, and Carnata, and their boys for trees—Oliver and Linden. Harold, sat in his favorite easy chair, next to the door to their closed-in front porch.

"We even tried to give it away," Harold said of their first attempts to sell what would become Mateskared to our family, "because we didn't want to pay the taxes on it." They paid $3 school tax and $8 land tax then. Harold knew exactly what they paid, because he was the collector for school taxes then. "Here now, school and land taxes are $2,000 a year," Harold said of their present home just down the hill from Mateskared.

Harold and Pansy had been asking $1,000 for what would become our family place up the hill. "Vernon Maxam had offered $600 or $700. In the meantime, Paul Schaefer came over and told Harold that Howard Zahniser would like to have the property and would give $1,000. Maxam was pretty upset and said that he would have come up to that." Paul Schaefer gave Harold $100 down to hold the property. "Howard Zahniser paid $1,000 for it but Paul Schaefer had already given me $100 down on it so I got $100 more than I was asking for it."

As Harold was talking, it struck me that the three of us were sitting and revisiting the Zahniser's Adirondack nesting advent in the very house—or at least part of the very house—to which Paul Schaefer first came to the Adirondacks. Paul's parents had rented the upstairs of the house Hugh Lackey then lived in on this very spot. Harold and Pansy's present house incorporates part of its Lackey structure. The elder Schaefers were here on doctor's orders for the relief of Paul's mother's seasonal allergies. The doctor had advised that another Schenectady city summer might do her in.

It wasn't completely true that my father "had never seen the place" before he bought the house Harold and Pansy had built on the portion they bought off her family's farm. On the last day of our family's first visit to the Adirondacks in August 1946, Paul took Zahnie for one last half-hour walk up the hill near the end of Edwards Hill Road out of Bakers Mills. Paul had said Zahnie owed him one last bit of conservation palaver. Three hours later, they returned by way of walking through Pansy and Harold's place adjacent to the top of the Dalaba's Hillmount Farms. At some point there, according to my father's journal of that summer, Paul and Zahnie stopped to admire the view down the valley toward Crane Mountain. If "the place" referred to the house but not its setting, then it would be true that Zahnie had seen only the exterior of the place.

Rooting through a box of family papers many years ago, I found the frantic August 13, 1946 letter Paul Schaefer wrote to Zahnie outlining the deal Harold Allen wanted for the place. The difference between the Maxam offer and my father's offer—and the reason Harold felt he could still take Zahnie's offer—was that my father was willing to take the 25-acre woodlot along with the six and a half-acre parcel with the Allen's house on it.

Paul urged my father to go for the woodlot, too: "If you can see your way clear, you couldn't miss by having both the house and the woodlot. One would make the other more valuable. Besides, they adjoin each other." Later in the letter Paul editorialized: "Of course I am personally thrilled at the prospect, as are my family and folks, but understand that such feeling as we have should not influence you one way or the other. But it really is I think the best buy I have yet seen up in that country."

It was entirely true that my mother Alice had never seen the place! There was a kitchen woodstove with water reservoir, a sheet iron stove in the downstairs living room/bedroom, and a hand water pump in the corner of the kitchen area. But neither stoves nor water pump conveyed with the property.

I remembered from my earliest years at Mateskared a hog pen, up behind the barn. By the time I remembered it, the pen was a fallen-down caricature of itself. Harold verified "a hog pen up above the barn on the edge of the woods." The edge of the woods now edges ever closer to our cabin.

When my parents bought the house and woodlot in late August 1946, the stairway was closed-in on just one side, and Pansy had a story about that. "Before it was completely sealed off, one Christmas Harold brought in a package, and he reached in between the floor and ceiling as far as he could reach. Now I was very inquisitive."

Pansy later snaked the package out with a hoe, looked at the contents, and put the package back in its hiding place. It was a beautiful pair of green fur and leather-palmed mittens.

"When I opened it Christmas morning, I was a bit of an actress," Pansy said.

"After I left up there," Harold said of selling our place to my parents and moving down the hill, "and even to this day, I sometimes think back to up there, because that was our first years of married life, and we did it all on no money." Harold backed up his no-money claim by saying that he didn't even have enough credit to buy a 15-cent file on credit at Harold Thistle's store in the nearby commercial center, North Creek.

"Harold Thistle's wife Roxie wouldn't give it to me on credit for 15 cents!" Harold said. He still seemed genuinely nonplused by the half-century-old denied transaction. Harold then recounted his working for the Works Project Administration (WPA) for one year.

"We got 40 dollars a month, paid once a month. I showed the check to Harold Dunkley, and he was so envious of it!" The largesse wasn't entirely rosy, especially with Harold's father in law. "John Dalaba called me a pauper for working for the WPA. He said that if he'd known I would be a pauper he wouldn't let Pansy marry me. To get on the WPA you had to get on town welfare and apply for an order of $10 to last for three weeks, but before that time was up, I got on WPA."

Pansy defended her choice of mate against that old specter of her father's anti-WPA wrath. Both her sister Daisy and her Aunt Esther Rist (Pansy's mother Hester's sister) subsequently married Allen men, Pansy pointed out. "They did it because they saw what a good job I did by marrying an Allen," Pansy said. Daisy's husband Earl was Harold's cousin.

Pansy came home to her parents' Hillmount Farms to have her first baby, and Harold and Pansy soon bought seven acres from John and Hester Dalaba for $300. Harold worked on the state road crew by then, and Pansy stayed with her parents a while. John Dalaba had people come help build the young couple's stone foundation. Harold G. Allen and his brother-in-law Harold Dunkley dug the foundation with a horse-drawn shovel. Some rocks for the fieldstone foundation were rolled up with a horse-drawn stone boat. It was John Dalaba's idea to use the gambrel-style roof, giving more room upstairs.

"We sold our pig—our meat for the winter—to buy the roofing material, tar paper with slate coating," Harold recalled. "We bought them from Ernest Noxon in North Creek."

Before they completed the house, Harold was drafted for World War II. "There was a big snowstorm that day," Harold said. It seemed to me he was now remembering a scene and not an event, as though the memory had its visual place marker. Although he could have gotten deferred, Harold said, "I had something to be fighting for." He and Pansy had three children by then. Harold went into the service in January 1943 and was discharged October 12, 1945. He had been stationed at an Air Force base that no longer exists.

Pansy's war took place here in Bakers Mills. "I stayed there with the three children," Pansy said. "Rats got in the house. It was the first time I screamed. I went down in the cellar and bumped the ceiling with a broom, and a rat ran down the broom and down my arm. I decided I needed a woodshed, and I put the boards out like I was going to do it." Then, mostly, John Dalaba and others came along, and they actually put it up.

Harold had built the barn in 1938. He tore down an old barn in the Willy Meadow—downhill and just east of Mateskared—that had belonged to William and Hattie Hitchcock. The couple had had a double wedding with Pansy's parents Hester Rist and John Dalaba. John was William's brother in law. The cowshed was built onto the south wall of the barn with $25 of lumber. It was delivered from Thurman—now part of the Glens Falls Metropolitan Statistical area—by the Baker sawmill man for whom Bakers Mills is named. Harold cut the shingles for the cowshed with his father's shingle machine, a saw table with alternate ends for tapering the shingles.

"We cut flat stones for Mateskared steps from the Willy place, too," Harold recalled. Both stones are still in use, although the stone they cut for the front door now serves one end of the cabin porch. added in 1967. Paul Schaefer's son Francis "Cub" Schaefer, Arnold McIntosh, and I added the porch in 1967.

"John Dalaba used to cut the hay in the Willy Meadow," Harold said. The whole interior upstairs of the house was made with flooring. Pansy did a lot of that herself while Harold was doing his WWII military service. Before that she used to hold up an Aladdin lamp with mantle on it there so Harold could see to work on the upstairs area.

"We thought we had a palace when we finished it," Harold said. "The house was 18 by 24 feet. The sills were made out of ash trees sawed by Uncle Del Allen from hardwood ash. A preacher from Canada was here holding services, and he helped build the house, and he showed us some of how to do things."

"When we moved into the house from my father's place with the new babies," Pansy said, "we had tarpaper on the floor over the rough lumber. That was hard to sweep." Their children Dody and Melvin were born in the front room, most of which is now a bedroom again.

Tapping into the Spring

"A property line in a woodland is an institution of strange and amusing aspects. Few of the activities in the woods recognize its shadowy authority."
—Walter Collins O'Kane

In the Harold and Pansy Allen family's e-mail newsletter *Dogtown News*, Harold once recounted how they got the water from the spring—which lies across the dirt road—into their first house, now our cabin named my parents named "Mateskared," I could tell Harold would repeat the tale despite my promising to read his e-zine account.

"Ranney was the proprietor of the Paul Schaefer Club property, the old club," Harold began, invoking the large block of land directly across road from our cabin. "I asked Archie Ranney if I could go over and pipe that water into the house. Ranney said 'Oh no. You cannot do that.' So I ignored what he said. I bought pipe and a pump from Ernest Noxon for $19.50. A week's wages then were $20.

"So I went at it and dug the ditch across the road and began to ditch it into the house. There was a stone I couldn't lift, so I used the car to lift it out in stages. Ranney came along and wanted to help, and he helped dig the stone out, and he never realized where the water was coming from—and he'd told me not to do it!"

"Harold had the pipe almost covered where it went across the road when Archie Ranney came up," Pansy interjected. "Archie would feed my baby fish off his plate, and I was scared about the bones."

"Archie was a man you could admire in many ways, but when he came to visit so often it became monotonous," Harold said. Daisy Allen's memoir *Ranger Bowback: An Adirondack Farmer* corroborates Harold's memory of Ranney.

About this same, time Ranney, whose nickname was "Bobcat," was trying to build a place back in the woods farther uphill, but he could not move a stone out of the foundation hole. Harold Allen and Harold Dunkley went up with a plank and moved it and didn't tell Ranney.

"Ranney never did find out how it got out of there, and we convinced him he had done it," Harold said.

That wasn't the only stunt Harold ever pulled at Ranney's expense. The usual Halloween Night trick here was to tip someone's outhouse over. Ranney had made it well known one Halloween that he would shoot anyone who came to tip his outhouse over.

That was too much of a challenge for Harold to ignore.

"My brother Arnold came over, and we decided to tip his outhouse over. Ranney had his gun on his lap and his dog Kess strapped to the outhouse. First, we went down and let the goat out of the house, and then we tipped the outhouse over.

The next morning Ranney was one mad man. He was going to have the police come and have somebody arrested. But Arnold and I decided to go back up and set it on its foundation just like we found it."

As to why Harold and Pansy sold the place up the hill to my parents: "We had to carry everything up there by hand in the winter time. And then we got the chance to buy this place." They moved in down the road here on Ground Hog Day, February 2, 1947. "This place was nice when I moved here," Harold recalled, and then added a bit of hyperbole: "It was a luxury hotel then." They had the property surveyed. It was 12 and 38/100ths acres.

"Now two kids have each taken an acre off it," Harold said, "and the taxes are the same!"

The first whole summer that our Zahniser family owned the cabin, we didn't go there. For our 1947 summer vacation, our family of six went out West for my father's work with The Wilderness Society. The Society's governing council's annual meeting was held that summer at the ranch of Olaus, President of the Society, and Mardy Murie at Moose, Wyoming. I was therefore curious to get Harold and Pansy's take on the history of our outhouse, whose provenance was conflicted in my memory.

"The outhouse was there," Pansy said definitively, meaning she and Harold built it. "It was a two-holer facing the barn and the woods." Their family used thunder mugs, chamber pots, inside the house. "They would freeze overnight," Pansy recalled dispassionately, "and you'd have to thaw them out in order to empty them."

"In the winter you couldn't get up that road in a car. Harold would carry 100-pound bags of grain up to feed the pigs. John Dalaba built that road with horses," Pansy said. She used her father's full name. "He built it so we could get a car over it. The town never took over that road while we lived there." Edwards Hill Road is now maintained by the Town of Johnsburg, a township of Warren County.

Not long after John Dalaba died in 1951, my parents Alice and Howard bought a few acres of Hillmount Farms just below our cabin. "Part of your barn is on me," John Dalaba had once confided to my father in the intimate language of a farmer who farmed as much with his hoe and footsteps as with his horse-drawn machinery. The southeast corner of the cowshed that Pansy and Harold built onto their small hay barn encroached on the Dalabas' 200-acre Hillmount Farm.

I have vivid memories, shared by my late sister Karen, of our father and Hester Dalaba walking the lines with her survey sheet in 1951 or 1952. Mrs. Dalaba needed to cleanup the ownership to transfer the farm to her church denomination as Camp Triumph. My parents wanted the cowshed that is attached to our barn entirely on our property. Its corner still sat on the Dalaba farm. They also wanted to give the cabin front more buffer space and to have the property generally make more sense visually. The twenty-five acres of woodlot Paul

Schaefer had urged my father to buy lay uphill. You couldn't stare at those acres out the cabin window.

"I remember feeling terribly sad after your momma bought that piece from momma," Pansy told me. "It had a beautiful blueberry chunk on it."

I later learned from reading Pansy's sister Daisy's book *Ranger Bowback: An Adirondack Farmer* that "chunk" meant any small plot of open land. Well into recent memory, Daisy's husband Earl still grew potatoes at the top of Camp Triumph, in what used to be his father-in-law's favorite potato chunk.

Pansy's beautiful blueberry chunk would now be in the recovering forest downhill from our cabin. Because the field has recovered to forest, and the trees have become so tall, we can no longer see Pansy and Harold's place from Mateskared. Pansy and Harold moved downhill and away from the wilderness in the mid-1940s. Today wildness has regained a great deal of ground on the hillside the young Allens left behind.

Letters of "Bobcat" Ranney and Howard Zahniser

Who comes to commend me on my way of life?
Well, the woodcutter sometimes passes by.
—Cold Mountain

Zahnie met Paul Schaefer and Schaefer's mentor John Apperson in February 1946 at the North American Wildlife Conference in New York City. There, Schaefer and Apperson showed their film about dam threats to Forest Preserve wilderness in the western Adirondacks. "The Wilderness Society Platform," in its item 9, stated:

"That encroachment upon our remnant American wilderness in any one locality is an attack upon the whole and creates an issue of national moment and not for local action alone."

Accordingly, at the conference, Zahnie offered Schaefer the Society's help to fight the series of dam proposals in what became known as the Black River Wars. Paul had suggested then that Zahnie and family visit the Schaefer family and their Adirondack camp off Edwards Hill Road out of Bakers Mills, New York, that summer.

The Ranney correspondence evidently begins, however, with a letter from Zahnie that Ranney refers to in his first letter, of July 23, 1946, whose envelope was addressed to Laurette Collier, Zahnie's half-time "assistant secretary" at The Wilderness Society's office at 1840 Mintwood Place, N.W., in the nation's Capital. (They were then the entire Washington office of the Society, which had been organized 11 years before.) Ranney's letter was posted from Bakers Mills on July 26. The Zahnisers' trip began that same day, so Zahnie would have seen the letter only after returning to the office in mid-August.

However, Ranney's handwritten letter, with handwritten attachment, opens by citing "Yours of the 19th inst[ant] reached me last night," evidently July 22. This suggests that Paul Schaefer earlier advised Ranney of Zahnie and family's trip, which began on July 26 and ended on their August 13 return to Maryland via Zahnie's mother's home in Tionesta, Pennsylvania, near where our parents are now buried beside the Allegheny River, and to which they had canoed in 1937 from Olean, New York.

Two entries in Zahnie's journal, published in *Where Wilderness Preservation Began: Adirondack Writings of Howard Zahniser* (North Country Books, 1992), record meetings with Ranney, as he was known. **Saturday August 3, 1946**. "Archie (Bobcat) Ranney and his visiting son came over to the porch and with Paul talked on the porch and told yarns. Mr. Ranney sang some of his mountain ballads,

and I read aloud some of Martha Keller's *Brady's Road and Other Ballads*."
Wednesday, August 7, 1946. "Just as we [Zahnie and older son Mathias] were starting for an overnight hike on Eleventh Mountain, Mr. Ranney came over to talk about Boy Scouts and to give me $1 for a Wilderness Society gift membership for Donald McCarty . . . a scoutmaster."

>Bakers Mills, N.Y.
>July 23, 1946

Howard Zahniser
Washington, D.C

Dear Mr. Zahniser
    Yours of the 19th inst reached me last night. I shall be indeed pleased to make you welcome to our mountain abode. Paul Schaefer has delegated me to regale you with some mountain music with my banjo-guitar and we can go into the subject of forestry and stream pollution to a more or less extent.
    Now don't be looking for a white-collared printer but rather a long-hair old billy goat who looks more like an Indian than a white man. But there is more than outside appearance in a man and a hermit must necessarily be an odd character.
    Living in this back district for the past 12 years, I seldom come in contact with city life but read quite extensively.
    As the time seems so short before you come to our north country, it seems best that I should defer acting as you suggest until your arrival.
    However, anything I can do to promote [sic] the further pollution and destruction of our forests and erosion of land, I shall indeed be glad of your suggestions thereto. [An attached newspaper clipping makes it clear that Ranney meant *prevent* not *promote*!]
    The enclosed clipping from the Binghamton Press will if the sewer is built help clean up a portion of the Susquehanna river.
    Our three-day rain found some leaks in my roof and some tarring will be in order as soon as the sun shines.
    They are no longer hiding bread under the counters but have upped the price to 14 cents per loaf. I had a porcupine for meat, over the week-end. One less bark-eater, at any rate.
>Sincerely, yours,
>Archie C Ranney

I live in the last house on Edwards Hill, two miles north of Bakers Mills. "The furder you go de tougher dey git."

Ranney appended to the letter his ballad, *The Tale of a Sourdough, Depicting Life In the Adirondacks as Experienced by Archie C. "Bobcat" Ranney. Composed and written on the eve of his 73rd Birthday, December 28, 1945.*

The next letter from Zahnie (below), dated September 20, 1946, exists as a yellow, second-sheet carbon copy. It may well be Zahnie's reply to the above letter from Ranney. Zahnie would receive the Honorary Doctor of Letters degree from his alma mater Greenville College in 1959. He told the convocation that he was so far behind in his correspondence that the degree should properly be called the "Doctor of Postcards."

September 20, 1946

Mr. Archie C. (Bobcat) Ranney,
Bakers Mills, Warren County, N.Y.

Dear Old Lynx:

With a carbon copy of this letter, our previous correspondence and your ballad "The Tale of a Sourdough" are going into the Wilderness Society files to await a resurrection on some sunny day (or rainy) when I get a chance to write something about the Adirondacks. You have become in my mind—not a correspondent to answer promptly—but a part of the Adirondacks along with Crane, Eleventh, Height-of-Land, and Gore. I think of all of you often, and I wish I could hear your banjo-guitar this afternoon.

For a month I have been hoping to get something written about your high spots up north, and I have kept your letter and ballad lying on the desk handy to the purpose. But now I'm giving up for the time being. Too much to do. But I want you to know how savory my recollections of the Adirondacks are and how much of the seasoning came from you.

Sincerely yours,
Howard Zahniser

P.S. I suppose you know that Alice and I bought Harold Allen's place, and the next time you see me you'll have to tolerate me as a neighbor. Who know[s], I might even some day aspire to succeed you as the Hermit of Cragorehol — even if I can't spell it yet.

—HZ

Bakers Mills, N.Y.
October 3, 1946, 3:15 p.m.

Mr. Howard Zahniser,
Washington, D.C.

My Dear Zahniser:

Welcome, indeed, to our Northlands. And the wife and kiddies also.

Two days and a night of snow and wind transformed our landscape into winter scenery.

Preceded by a day's rain, much of it melted. I estimate six inches of snow fell here. Other sections, farther north, 12 inches. It cleared off during last night and the sun has left the ground bare and green.

My condition seems to be improving. I now walk to Hitchcock's for milk and sit up a greater part of the day. The leg ulcers are healing slowly.

Secured a bottle of Zanex, the army remedy for Athletics' feet, consisting of iodine, sal[i]cyllic acid, boric acid in alcohol. That should kill the germs and help heal the ulcers. An Endicott Scoutmaster sent it to me as his good turn, Dominick Rossi. Rossi is a fine Italian, much interested in nature study. He is employed at the Endicott post office, since his army discharge.

As for becoming a part of the Adirondacks, I am indeed deeply rooted here. I have much in common with the natives here, having fished, hunted, slept in the woods and camps with them, eaten in their homes and shared their joys and sorrows.

My great-grandfather, Captain John Marsh, of Or[o]no, Maine was Indian interpreter to the Massachusetts legislature for the Penobscot tribe of Indians, was adopted into the tribe by all the rites of blood brotherhood and the Indians gave him Arumsunkhumgen (Marsh Island) in the Penobscot river, containing 5,000 acres of fertile land for 30 bushels of corn and other considerations. My grandfather, Jeremiah Marsh, was a Maine circuit rider. Indians visited our home in Maine. I can just remember being afraid of a squaw who came selling baskets and mats to our home. Great grandfather married Sarah Colburn, the fair haired daughter of a miller to whom he sold mill rights on the island. My grandfather John Ranney, a Lowland Scot, emigrated to New Ireland, Canada, and later brought his family to Northern Vermont. My father moved there after his marriage and after I was born went to the Dodlin stone quarries in Kenduskeag, Me., as a tool dresser. I left my Vermont home at the age of 9 years, with my mother, to live in Athens, Pa.

I early acquired a thirst for adventure and in the outdoors found my greatest pleasure. From these tendencies I became known as the Indian of the Marsh family among my mother's kin.

Then, is it any wonder that in my latter days I have sought the solitude of the last vestiges of the once great forests I have seen hewn down and destroyed by the ruthless axe of man?

As the Hermit of Dogtown (Bakers Mills) I hope to hold forth until The Great Spirit of the Universe shall call me to the Happy Hunting Grounds — and a worthy successor, such as yourself, take my place, to carry on the fight for the preservation of the last remaining vestiges of our once rich forest heritage.

With my best regards to your wife and the dear little kiddies, I remain
Sincerely yours
Archie C. "Bobcat" Ranney

P.S. — John Dalaba saw a large black bear last week in his back lot. When the bear saw John he ran for the tall timbers.

Leaves are turning to glorious fall colors as the scarlet maple, wild cherries, etc., but few have fallen as yet.

John Hitchcock dug a Green Mountain potato last week. Annie [Hitchcock] cooked the knobs on it for supper and had some left over besides three pounds of the main potato. Some tater, what.

The above letter appears to be the last correspondence between Ranney and Zahnie.

About 1950 or 1951, as our family and Grace Oehser paused our car below our steep, dirt approach road to Mateskared, Ranney joined us from his nearby cabin. Ranney was by then what we called "stone deaf." His hearing disability caused Grace Oehser to lie about her age — and to lie *upward* not downward, as is often one's wont. She was in her late 40s but finding it impossible to communicate her specific, three- or four-syllable age to Ranney. Exasperated, she yelled at the top of her lungs "FIFTY!" Ranney got it.

In those days, we sometimes had to get a running start to get our car up the steep part of the dirt road to our cabin. In my father's attempt to express this need to Ranney, he pulled out his blue-leaded editorial pencil, made a quick, freehand upward-slanting line on a sheet of paper, and yelled "LIKE A BLUE STREAK!" Ranney got that, too.

Many years after Ranney's death, Carolyn Schaefer and son Francis "Cub" and youngest daughter Monica; my friend Larry Strausbaugh and I; and Don Oehser essayed to clean out Ranney's cabin. We didn't get very far. Carolyn entertained thoughts of fixing it up to rent out to skiers. We found a box of strike-anywhere "safety" matches that Cub was insistent be removed from the cabin, because rats could chew their tips and start a fire. Ranney's cabin has now disappeared not only from view but also from the material plane, in the inexorable recovering vegetation of Adirondack land formerly kept open by grazing, haying, or agriculture.

The Oehser Camp and Fred West

*How could someone who practices not become a Buddha
if water drips long enough even rocks wear through*
—Stonehouse

Grace Edgbert and Paul Oehser were college chums of my father Howard in the 1920s at Greenville College in western Illinois. Grace and Paul subsequently married, and after graduation Paul took a job as an editor with the U.S. Department of Commerce in Washington, D.C. Paul eventually convinced Zahnie to move to the Washington area as a federal editor, too.

Zahnie had arrived at college on crutches because of a surgery in his teens for the degenerative bone disease, osteomyelitis. The disease was considered 50-percent fatal then. Because he didn't know whether he would live to graduate, Greenville College administrators allowed him to take whatever courses he wanted. He ignored several required courses. Still alive after four years, Zahnie lacked a year's worth of requirements. He spent a fifth year as a hybrid freshman and sophomore in order to be graduated.

"I crammed four years of college into five!" was the spin he put on his academic career.

After graduation, my father worked for a year as a reporter on the *Pittsburgh Press* newspaper. The next year he edited the town of Greenville's *Advocate* newspaper, and then taught high school English for a year there. During his college years and after, his father was Pastor of Town and Gown Free Methodist church for a three-year stint in the late 1920s.

In 1929, Paul Oehser convinced Zahnie to take the Civil Service exam when it was next offered in nearby St. Louis. Zahnie did and passed it. He arrived in Washington, D.C., on New Year's Eve 1929, not such a hayseed as to think wildly ringing bells were just for him. He went to work in the Commerce Department's editorial operation alongside Oehser. Their boss was the precise and meticulous Chief Editor Mr. Cheesman. Commerce then included the Bureau of Fisheries.

William Cheesman must have mentored his young staff well. He would finish his government career working for my father, and Paul Oehser would become Chief of Publications for the Smithsonian Institution, writing its history as the book *Sons of Science.* Importantly for me, Paul and Grace became my mentors in all things artistic and literary, especially after my father died when I was an 18-year-old freshman at Greenville College.

Paul was an editor and poet and later helped establish public television in the Washington, D.C. area. Grace was an artist. She not only white-washed Mateskared's first-floor interiors, but she painted with oils and watercolors and did wood-block printing. She has work in the collections of The Adirondack Museum and The Smithsonian. Grace illustrated my first book of Adirondack poems, *The Way to Heron Mountain*, and a later chapbook of poems, *Sheenjek and Denali: Alaska Poems*. She also encouraged my writing, whether poetry or prose. In the 1970s, I dedicated at least two one-off, hand-written and drawn books to her.

My first memories of Mateskared are from our family's first summer stay there in 1948. My memories reflect fix-up work done by Grace Oehser, their younger teenaged son Dick, and his friend Fred West in summer 1947. My parents bought the future Mateskared after our first Adirondack sojourn in 1946. I had stayed behind with an aunt in Washington, D.C. Our whole family then spent summer 1947 in Moose, Wyoming, with Margaret E. "Mardy" and Olaus Murie. We stayed at their former dude ranch spread in full and glorious view of the Grand Teton. The ranch and its Murie Center are now part of Grand Teton National Park.

Olaus served as director of The Wilderness Society then, a half-time job set up in Fall 1945 as Zahnie was hired as the Society's executive secretary and magazine editor. At that reorganization meeting, Benton MacKaye, founder of the Appalachian Trail, became the Society's president. Ecologist and wildlife scientist Aldo Leopold became vice president.

"What is our function in this the post-war period we are entering?" MacKaye had asked the Society's governing council—rhetorically, it turns out—in one of his six letters that primed his colleagues for the reorganization meeting. "Is it big or little? If 'little' we should liquidate. But I am assuming it is 'big'—if for no other reason than the condition of our average returning fighter from [World War II]—his need for a place wherein serenity shall quell confusion." That place was wilderness.

The Society's long-time Treasurer Ernest Griffith later said the reorganization caucus was "probably the most important meeting the Society has ever held." It had taken place in Washington, D.C., in July 1945.

The 1947 annual board meeting of the Society's governing council was to be held in late summer at the Murie's ranch. It was to include a packtrip with horses into the Cloud Peak Primitive Area of Wyoming's Bighorn Mountains northeast of the Tetons and east of Yellowstone National Park. Zahnie, Olaus, and Mardy worked ahead in Moose on meeting preparations.

It would prove to be a historic meeting—if only in retrospect—because the Society's governing council formally voted to make a push for some form of statutory protection for wilderness at the federal level. That push would take eight more years to launch. It would take another eight years to succeed. But that 1947 vote set my father's career destiny as author and constant advocate of the federal wilderness legislation that became the 1964 Wilderness Act.

Grace Oehser's 1947 interior painting work at Mateskared was whitewashing. She mixed the whitewash powder and water, then brushed it onto the walls and ceiling of the cabin's downstairs rooms. "Whitewashing" has become a term for a cover-up, but Grace's job brightened up the cabin interior. As to the Mateskared environs, the family myth seems to have been that Grace's son Dick and his friend Fred West built our outhouse. At least for many decades, I somehow held that impression. Fred later worked with a prominent architectural firm headquartered in Georgetown, in Washington, D.C. It makes a fine story, or myth even, to have the primitive privy built in part by a future accomplished architect.

Unfortunately, that is not how Fred, who lived in Great Falls, Virginia, remembered it.

"There was a privy, perched downhill at a rakish angle." Fred recalled for me several years before he died. "Under the circumstances, its state of disrepair seemed unremarkable and my recollection of working with Dick to restore its utility is no stronger than that of sweeping out the house or chopping the weeds."

Fred also remembers its lack of a door—which lack continues to this day—as something of a challenge to conventional modesty "given the presence of a female." But "Grace introduced the protocol of the 'occupancy flag' to preclude awkward social encounters," according to Fred. "The flag of course meant nothing to porcupines that doubtless continue to alarm privy patrons with pointedly anti-social encounters." Well, only at night, a fact attributable more to the porcupine's nocturnal habits rather than to his or her inability to see the occupancy flag in the dark. A flag, often a red bandanna, still flies in summer.

"That the accommodations we found teetered between spartan and ramshackle," Fred recollected of his summer of 1947, "was of little moment given the idyllic nature of the landscape and the whole enterprise. Indeed, to a nineteen-year-old enamored of camping, the arrangement seemed ideal: dipping water from a spring, cooking on an open fire, sleeping on the floor with assorted vermin, perfection itself."

I was comforted by Fred's reminiscences. For years I had told other members of my family that Fred's aunt lived somewhere near Mateskared. Sometimes they doubted me. Fred confirms the uncanny coincidence of his high school friend Dick Oehser—they both lived in Arlington, Virginia then—telling him the Oehser's family friends, the Zahnisers, had just bought a cabin and some land on the edge of nowhere and actual wilderness in Bakers Mills, New York, a two-day drive then from their northern Virginia suburb of Washington, D.C.

"Oh yeah? Edge of *nowhere,* my foot!" I can imagine Fred challenged Dick. "That's where my great-aunt Rosa lives. I've been there *lots* of times."

"My first visit on Edwards Hill was in 1934 or 1935 with my mother and sister at the house of my great-aunt Rosa Roitner," Fred said. "I can still call up the wonderful amalgam of odors in that house—wood smoke, drying herbs, German cooking. And the one piece of plumbing, the kitchen sink, consisting of a sloping trough of galvanized steel draining mysteriously into an under-house pit, with the water supplied by a hand pump. That summer, too, I met Archie Ranney, not yet a total recluse, who would visit my aunt now and again."

Fred remembers Ranney wearing "remnants from the Spanish-American War—campaign hat, button-front tunic, puttees—but this may be pure romantic imagination." By the time of my earliest memories of a bearded Bobcat Ranney, Fred West had known of him for fifteen years or more.

Fred also remembers: "My aunt hooked hand-size trout from her brook at sunrise to be served for breakfast." That would be the Cold Spring Brook I fished in the late 1950s and early 1960s. It turns out Fred fished it in the 1930s. He sent me an old photo to prove it. When my brother Matt and I took my young sons back into Cold Spring Brook, inactive beaver dams made access difficult, and fishing nearly impossible. We caught a few chubs.

So, architect Fred West did not build the outhouse in summer 1947 but only helped perfect its rakish tilt later. Grace Oehser's 1947 interior cabin work was still working fine when, some 20 summers later, when I was in the U.S. Army in South Korea, my mother asked Earl Allen to redo the fireplace room's walls and ceiling with knotty pine. Our childhood home in Maryland was a goner then. Earl's pine boards my mother relined our mother's replacement nest, Mateskared.

Paul and Grace Oehser were both born a few years before my father's birth in 1906. Paul (1904–1996) once told me about his first paying work as a youngster. He picked blackberries for a penny a quart in western New York's agricultural landscape of small, family-operated farms. Grace Edgbert (1902–1999) grew up in Wisconsin, where the recent aftermath of logging's great sweep westward still manifested in the abundance of blackberries. Logging set back the forest succession clock. Logging was often followed then by terrible fires—raging through the helter-skelter slash aftermath—that set back the successional clock even further. Grace has often shared her growing-up tales of blackberry bounty with us. After Mateskared's hillside succeeded beyond easy blackberry wealth, she would invite us to pick the Oehser's more recently cow-free fields.

Grace and Paul bought their camp in the mid-1950s. They too had fallen in love with the Adirondacks and no longer were content with working their love of the place into our family's nesting schedule at Mateskared. They found a foothills plot of land just around the Bakers Mills corner of Eleventh Mountain from Mateskared. Their real estate was improved by a cabin, very small barn outbuilding, and pit-styled outhouse. For many years after the Oehsers bought the camp, their neighbor farmer Johnny Steve ran his cows on their fields by agreement. It could be unnerving to step out on their porch in the morning to be greeted by a cow standing with its head over the railing.

Johnny Steve started out more protective of the place than neighborly to its new owners. The first night Grace and Paul spent in the cabin after clinching the sale, Johnny Steve showed up after dark, armed, and ordered the pajamaed couple to vacate the premises at once. He thought they were flatlander squatters, not new owners. Fortunately, Paul had brought a copy of the deed. Once a suspicious Johnny even consented to look at the deed, he was reluctantly convinced the place had indeed changed hands without his knowing it.

Grace and Paul's cabin was not organic to their camp. It had arrived there in two pieces from elsewhere long before they bought the place. It came complete with a nicely hand-painted sign betraying its former life—whole—as the Doug Morehouse Hunting Club. Doug Morehouse grew up on Edwards Hill Road. Paul Schaefer described him "the acknowledged leader of the guides in the area."

From his former hunting club, Doug Morehouse guided parties into the Flow of Second Pond Brook, in the wilderness four and a half miles beyond Mateskared. During hunting season Doug kept large canvas tents set up at the Flow. This large flat grassy meadow, now episodically worked by beavers is an artifact of the logging era. Loggers once dammed it so the impounded waters could be used to "flow" spruce logs downstream out of the wilderness during the high, spring runoff. Second Pond Brook is tributary to the East Branch of the Sacandaga River. Many times I have stone-hopped up and down this small outlet to the Flow while fishing. You would not dream that loggers once flushed big saw logs down it to market. The Flow is now part of the Siamese Ponds Wilderness.

By the early 1960s, Grace settled on naming their place Camp Hardway. Despite its pit-styled outhouse, Camp Hardway seemed plush by Mateskared standards, with its wood cooking range complete with baking oven and its well with hand-pump right off the front porch. I tried to convince Grace to call their place Chalet Hardway but no go. This was after cows no more grazed its fields, and the fields began to succeed to brush and saplings that began to crowd out the abundant blackberries. How much the berry plants bespoke nostalgia for Grace's Wisconsin girlhood I can only now begin to guess, now that both my childhood and its Mateskared blackberry stage of succession have now passed.

Block print of Edwards Hill Road from Route 9 northward with an image representing our cabin at the top. It was made by the late Grace Oehser. Grace and husband Paul were college chums of my father. Grace has a couple of artworks in the permanent collection of the Adirondack Museum, if memory serves me right. The Oehsers eventually bought a place off Route 8, just around the south end of Eleventh Mountain from our family's Mateskared cabin on Edwards Hill Road.

Porcupine Deconstructs Landscape Art

*I think of the leek growing in the garden.
Day after day people pull off the leaves,
But the heart it was born with stays the same.*
—Cold Mountain

There is now no cow anywhere along Edwards Hill Road, only cow parts in freezers. The late Earl Allen kept two draft horses into the 21st century, but he modernized his sugar bush's bungs and buckets with a network of plastic piping. Earl's horses used to see the deep woods in late fall, when Earl packed hunting parties into camp in what is now the Siamese Ponds Wilderness. For decades, Earl packed for Paul Schaefer's hunting party, the Cataract Club. Earl had inherited the job from his father-in-law Big John Dalaba.

As landscapes, Mateskared and the Adirondacks resist change by virtue of human memory. The rising tide of vegetation surrounding the Acting Rock does not change the rock's name or significance for me. It may give my sons Justin and Eric a different set of memories, or little in the way of memories. Maybe they've never heard someone declaim from its summit. Maybe they've never perched on it fearfully, as their older cousin Layla Ward remembers doing. She remembers being fearful that she might tumble down the rock's backside. There, the imposing mass of vegetation was "over her head."

It gets even more complex. When our son Justin was not yet three months old, Christine and I brought him from West Virginia to Mateskared. What with nursing and other travails of travel with a baby, we made the eleven-hour trip in just sixteen-hours. After everyone else had gone to bed, I sat against the wall opposite the cabin fireplace. I had an ineffable sense of my father's presence. He had died seventeen years before. But there he sat at the southeast corner desk, the desk that had not been there since Paul Schaefer cut in our picture window three years after my father died.

Memorial artifacts—I don't know what else to call them—exist not only in the cabin but in the landscape. Sometimes they exist out of synch with the so-called facts, which are other people's memories. Or they are the facts of photographs, or the facts confused by photographs, or recalled images of old photographs now lost.

Does an apparently erroneous memory, once so-called "corrected," then cease to exert influence on the present? Or at least on the present *landscape*—a term whose etymology emanates from the German *landscaft*, which, as historian Simon Schama writes, "signified a unit of human occupation." The word worked into English via the Netherlands' *landscap*.

Memory definitely attaches to depictions of landscapes. An oil painting Grace Oehser rendered in the early 1950s was later briefly in my possession. Grace painted the view from Mateskared, looking toward Eleventh Mountain. The view depicted is now a historic vista. You can no longer see what Grace painted. Successional tree growth has blocked our former viewshed of the mountain's lower elevations from Mateskared.

But neither view nor painting alone invokes my memory.

Grace had been working on the painting downhill from the cabin. It was all but finished. She decided to let the oils paints dry overnight in the barn. That was our childhood rainy-day play spot. It was dry and close enough to the cabin for parental purview out of earshot. Much to Grace's chagrin, the next morning, a porcupine had gnawed a hole in her painting. Evidently, the porky tried the taste of oil paints with a high-fiber side dish of canvas.

Grace's style was not so archly realistic that you'd speculate the porcupine had fancied eating a poplar tree depicted in the painting. This quilled connoisseur showed good taste in faithfully wrought landscape art. He or she also seemed to appreciate aesthetic distance. But eating fine art would not come into vogue until the 1960s art happenings.

Grace's painting stands on its own merits—only from the backside can you discern her sewn, canvas-patching job. Grace's paintings are also held in the permanent collection of the Adirondack Museum at Blue Mountain Lake. But for me, no painting is so quintessentially Mateskared as this view of Eleventh Mountain that a wild porcupine found good enough to eat.

The Cellar and Past Neighbors Uphill

Memories seem to us like messages from a past whose author isn't quite the self we know. They have a position similar to dreams in the sense that they are visited upon us.
— Kay Ryan, Synthesizing Gravity.

"Don't step too far back in the pantry or you might fall into the cellar," our mother Alice used to admonish us kids at Mateskared. Foreboding powers seemed to emanate from our dirt-floored fieldstone cellar walled by the cabin's foundation.

When I was very young the cellar lurked dungeon-like, unlit, mostly unseen below, and haunted with that adult admonition. Its night version—*"Howard! What's that noise in the kitchen?"*—audibly whispered by our mother from the downstairs bedroom split the pitch-dark, timeless expanse of childhood cabin nights. Our mother feared animals' getting into the cabin from the cellar.

We needed no precociousness for Jungian psychology to project psychic content onto the lumpy, dirt-floored, always dark, dank, sometimes wet root cellar. We could enter it only by stooping though a low, crude, half-height door below the front of the cabin or, in early years, via the foreboding back of the pantry off the kitchen. The latter required a spooky descent by a rickety, narrow-tread, open stairway.

In the mid-1950s, my mother would commission our carpenter neighbor Ernie Hitchcock to floor the pantry stairs opening with thick plywood. Hardly projecting her Shadow, Mom wanted to quit worrying that any cabin kitchen night noise might mean a raccoon or rat had gotten in through the fieldstone cellar.

Pansy and Harold Allen, who built our place, stored potatoes in the cellar, root crops from their kitchen garden, apples, and canned items subject to freezing. As agriculture increases in latitude and altitude—and especially both—potatoes often loom large among crops. Even into the 1950s, some Adirondack families still might greet springtime eating a constrained diet of last year's potatoes and the new year's early peas.

The Dalaba family grew potatoes in more than one field below our cabin. Their fields were laboriously cleared of stones and rocks that could be removed by hand or with their team of horses. Indeed, potatoes can seem like analogous rocks, *les roches de la terre,* to be dug out in perpetuity as frost-heaving yearly surfaced new crops of rock.

The potato originated in the Americas, in Peru. Witness how the French name for potato literally means "apple of Earth," *pomme de terre.* The analogy acknowledges that apples, originally from Central Asia, preceded potatoes in Europe. In France and England, what we Americans call "French fries" are literally "fried apples," *pommes frites.* The apple came to America from Europe. This exchange was among the eventual outcomes of Christopher Columbus' encounters with a few islands in the Caribbean and off the coast of North America. Columbus never set foot on the Americas' mainland.

Mateskared sits at 2,100 feet of elevation, staring across at Crane Mountain, whose summit is 3,254 feet above sea level. A tabloid displayed in the nearby town of North Creek's supermarket once advised: "Sea level rising 150 feet." We would be safe at Mateskared—as long as we required nothing of New York, Boston, Los Angeles, Seattle, the whole of South Florida, or much of Washington, D.C.

Because Mateskared lies pitched on the hill slope of Height of Land mountain at 2,100 feet of elevation, we enjoy a generally longer frost-free growing season than Bakers Mills, two miles away, at 1,594 feet of elevation. Mountains generate air movement, a phenomenon known as orographic winds. Warming air currents rise in the morning and cooler air moves falls toward evening. "Frost pockets" occur where cold downdrafts deposit colder air. Paul Schaefer's daughter Evelyn and husband Don Greene used to garden at the old Putnam Farm at the base of Crane Mountain. One summer they had a maximum of 21 growing days between killing frosts.

The fact that still more hardscrabble subsistence farms once stood farther above us here on Edwards Hill boggles the mind. I asked the late Reverend Daisy Dalaba Allen about them. Daisy was Pansy's sister and married to Earl, who was Pansy's husband Harold's cousin. Earl made maple syrup. I was down at their place for a visit and to pick up our annual syrup ration.

Daisy recalled at least three more farms above Mateskared but said they would have been gone by 1939, when her sister Pansy and husband Harold began building their home which became ours.

When I was a young teenager, a man with the roads commission came up our hill on a tractor mounted with a sickle bar. He said he was a Hitchcock and talked of a relative once farming above us, up the road. The road as a road now ends at Mateskared but once continued straight up beside our cabin for about 400 feet. It then made a right angle turn toward Sodom, New York. Mr. Hitchcock told me his folks carried their drinking water uphill from our spring—no mean feat. A gallon of water weighs more than 8 pounds, and you wouldn't trek down that hill for just one gallon.

Daisy recalled that the road once continued beyond Chatiemac eastward to Barton Mines, the former garnet mines on the far side of our near back neighbor Gore Mountain. (At Barton Mines, someone had in 1828 found economic sustenance from Adirondack rocks. Local garnet is still in demand for industrial abrasives.) When Daisy said that, I seemed to recall having seen an early 1930s topographical map that showed the old road going through to the hamlet of Sodom. Sodom is now a crossroads with a small, cut stone former schoolhouse near where Peaceful Valley Road splits off Route 8 about halfway between Bakers Mills and Johnsburg. Daisy's husband Earl countered that he doubted the road ever went on to Sodom.

As it turns out, Earl Allen was wrong, a rare occurrence in my experience. Recently, cartographer Tom Patterson pointed me to a US Geological Survey website of old topographical maps. Indeed, an 1898 Thirteenth Lake Quadrangle map shows the old road going through to Sodom. The map also shows that today's Chatiemac Road to Chatiemac Lake did not exist then.

I can locate two former home sites above Mateskared. One stood just north of where Edwards Hill Road makes its right-angle turn toward Sodom. Another, evidently smaller place stood a half-mile or less east of the turn. The former used to be clearly marked by its huge lilac bushes. The latter was evidenced by a shallow cellar dent and a few less-than-random rock placements. I could imagine the dwellings but not their inhabitants' sustenance from these thin soils.

Fence Full of Car Parts in Bakers Mills

*A few good things are left on earth
And they are not manufactured.
—Paul Blackburn*

My older brother Matt and I recently reminisced about the residents of Bakers Mills and Edwards Hill Road in the 1950s. They possessed a vast range of skills and competencies that we, as suburbanites, so sorely lacked. They had "can do" reactions to most any situation, however daunting it might have seemed to Matt and me. Their first thought was not to "look up" how-to instructions. The following anecdote, courtesy of David Gibson, Managing Partner of Adirondack Wild, Friends of the Forest Preserve, illustrates what Matt and I had marveled about. The anecdote originally ran in the "Adirondack Almanack," John Warren blogmeister. It is offered here with Gibson's kind permission.

Paul Schaefer (1908-1996) had loads of stories to tell about his life and the people he came to know in the Adirondacks.

Now that Adirondack rivers are starting to flow again and trout season is about to open, it may be an appropriate time to relay one Paul told me at his fireside.

Folks living where Paul had his Adirondack camp were, and still are, very resourceful people and equally ready to help someone in need, so this story has the ring of truth. (Paul was not always comfortable being recorded, so I tried to capture his stories in a small tape recorder in my car on the way home).

Paul split his time between the Adirondacks and his family's home and his home construction business in Schenectady County. He was known as an able Adirondack guide for "sports," men from the city who wanted to fish or hunt. One day in the 1940s a Schenectady neighbor said "Paul, I have a real hankering to go fishing. Boy, I'd love to get a creel full of fish. I hear the East Branch of the Sacandaga has beautiful brookies, and boy it would be great if you would bring me there to fish."

"Well, how about now?" answered Paul, and off they went to Bakers Mills. From there they hiked through the woods to the East Branch of the Sacandaga River where they caught creels of brook trout, one of the most successful days Paul ever had.

Loaded with fish, they hiked out, got in Paul's car and headed toward Bakers Mills. They only made a few hundred yards when they heard a grinding sound at the back axle. Paul's friend determined they had broken a critical gear on the rear axle, a small gear seemingly made just for that car.

Just then George Morehouse came over with a "what's the trouble, boys?"

"This critical gear is broken and these fish are going to spoil if we don't get them home. We've got to get home tonight," Paul's friend said.

"Well, hold on, boys," answered George, going to a fence along the road where all sorts of radiators, hoses, fan belts, gears and such which he had picked off the road for decades were hanging. In a trice, he was back with the particular gear. "This what you're looking for?" Paul's friend's jaw dropped. The gear fit perfectly and they drove on back to Schenectady.

'Part of Your Barn Is on Me'

Who can break from the snares of the world
And sit with me among the white clouds?
—Cold Mountain

Big John Dalaba was a farmer, and he spoke about his land as himself. Not long before he died in 1951, he and our father Howard stood looking out at the view of Crane Mountain from our cabin, which Big John's daughter Pansy and husband Harold Allen built. Our cabin sits on part of the Dalaba Hillmount Farm that Big John and his wife Hester had deeded to Pansy and Harold as a wedding gift in 1938. But one corner of our cowshed that Harold and Pansy had built onto their barn still sat on the Dalaba property when my parents bought Mateskared in 1946.

"Part of your barn is on me," I overheard Big John confide to my father—as neighbor talk, not assertion of ownership. He still ran his cows on our place until August, then when he would fence the cows out of our cabin space.

As the former pastureland uphill behind the cabin gradually recovered from grazing, blackberry bushes flourished in prodigious numbers. Berry picking was our chore as children. We ate the berries on oatmeal or "cold cereal," or in blackberry fried pies our mother Alice cooked over wood fires—indoors or out—for our summer lives without electricity or running water. The spring was both water supply and refrigerator then, raided sometimes by raccoons or black bears. In those early years, the hamlet of Bakers Mills—two miles down Edwards Hill Road on Route 8—had a general store with gas pump and post office. Now, only a post office remains.

After Big John Dalaba died, his widow Hester sold my parents a piece of land to correct that encroaching cowshed problem, making it "sit on us" now. Until recently our late parents' grandchildren and great grandchildren also vacationed here, some sleeping in tents in the yard or barn. With the offspring of Alice and Howard Zahniser now greatly proliferated, the cabin is far too small and its potential for cooking large meals too limited. We must now avail ourselves of multiple summer rentals farther down Edwards Hill Road.

Stray things still roost in memory from the annals of our former summer world. At Thanksgiving, the Dalaba family ritually dined on oysters not turkey. And Big John Dalaba called his potato field his potato "chunk." Pansy Allen mourned the disappearance of her favorite "blueberry chunk." By the mid-1950s, former habitations uphill from Mateskared were identifiable only by out-sized lilac bushes or by what Henry David Thoreau wrote about as "cellar dents," shallow impressions of former root cellars where dwellings once stood.

My sole surviving sibling Mathias and I can still share many such things almost without speaking.

What Hugh Lackey Told Paul Schaefer

*". . . for no world is possible without verticality,
and that dimension alone
is enough to evoke transcendence."* —Mircea Eliade

Mateskared cabin sits on a level spot no more natural to the topography than is the electric pole next to the John, our outhouse. The cutbank below the garden, from which Dave and I scabbed sand for mortar, is a tip-off. When Pansy and Earl built this place in the late 1930s, they created the level spot by cutting into the slope and then filling out around the foundation. The foundation became a fieldstone retaining wall at the front, lower aspect of the natural slope. A brief, soil deck at the front of the cabin is now covered by the porch we added to Mateskared in 1967.

This soil deck was created by a second, dry fieldstone wall just downhill of the cabin foundation's front wall. Like a huge stone planter or crib, it runs the length of the cabin front and extends out about six feet. The walled, earthen island a platform to access the front door and helped stabilize the foundation. It also insulated the cellar's crucial winter storage of apples and potatoes and other root crops. A gap through this artificial island gave access to the exterior cellar door.

The pervasive Adirondack shortage of level land is well expressed in the concept of the hereafter held by the old guide Hugh Lackey. Lackey once asked the young Paul Schaefer what he thought heaven would be like. Paul just swept his arm around at the surrounding countryside and said "something like this," heaven on Edwards Hill Earth.

Not so for Lackey.

"Lots of times I get to thinking if I could have a hundred flat acres of land to till, why I wouldn't care how almighty hard the Boss made me work!" the old guide said. "That would be my idea of a fine place."

Not that Lackey didn't love the home place, level or not.

"I just couldn't leave this here country," he confided to Paul. "Even those blasted rocks seem so friendly at times!"

Earl Allen did major repairs to the cabin's foundation and sills many years ago. As the foundation shifted, the cabin bowed, perhaps a bit like Noah's ark might have. Frost action in this climate can be spectacular. Major rocks get thrust up through road surfaces or cause them to welt, buckle, and heave. Frost action and alternate freezing and thawing as deep snow melts away are enemies of Adirondack real estate.

To keep the root cellar from freezing you had to keep the living space above it heated or at least keep it from cooling down for too long. In our mobile age with thermostat-controlled central heating, it's hard to fathom the stay-putness required to keep uninsulated space warm for long winters with frequent subzero weather. But nearby Bakers Mills was a full-service community then, with a general store with gas pumps and post office.

When I was a young child, John and Lillian Morehouse ran the general store, a suburban child's dreamscape of candies, notions, multiple bins of all manner of nails and tacks and screws, basic hand tools, rudimentary fishing tackle, boots, caps, bandannas, sewing patterns, utensils, and more, in addition to meats, dairy products, produce, and other consumables in cans and cartons. Especially enticing were large sugar cookies purveyed singly in bins not in cellophaned packs of half dozens. On a kid's economy of scale, the choice to buy just one cookie can be the only hope of buying one's own cookie. Today, cookies cost so much they again sell as singles but individually wrapped.

Just so was the foundation of a root cellar once wedded to a community's foundation.

Now we have the potential for central heating, but if you need a nail, you must go to Wevertown (6 miles), North Creek (9 miles), Warrensburg (20 miles), or Glens Falls (35 miles). Glens Falls now boasts that most modern of all miracles, an enclosed shopping mall. But I would enjoy the option of walking two miles from our cabin to Bakers Mills and its general store—in good weather! That one's own footsteps should carry one to such source and supply would be a firm foundation for a way of life.

While house and barn timbers were often fashioned from peeled logs, the cowshed was tightly built of rough-sawn, two-by-four lumber sheathed with rough-sawn boards. Lapped wooden shingles covered them. The cowshed had a poured slab floor on its fieldstone foundation, with a poop trough that ran out through the east wall. Plush construction reflected how a few milk cows could be a young family's largest capital investment after the real estate itself. Protecting cows from the elements also reduced demand for feed, and hay was limited by the amount of cleared land.

When I was 16 years old, I pulled out the cowshed stanchions, boarded up the opening into the barn, and built shutters for its two small, three-pane windows. I built a sleeping loft of salvaged beams, floored with purchased white-pine boards. Soon, I added a table and chairs. I calculated that after college I could live in the cowshed year-round with no car for about $600 a year. Obviously, I was not planning on college and a major in economics—or for health and life insurance, retirement pension, or the cable TV, satellite dish, and Internet hookups, not yet invented then. My dreams were inspired by the poured-slab floor and how three sides of the cowshed were weather tight and could be readily insulated.

I measured the cowshed often. It was commodious compared to Thoreau's small cabin at Walden Pond. No doubt, by the end of my first winter there, it might feel like a telephone booth. More recently, the cowshed's poured concrete slab has shifted and started breaking up like river ice at spring break-up, or like Earth's tectonic, crustal plates.

My consolation as my youthful dreams crack and tilt is that I can no longer envision living at Mateskared for $600 a year. Each year my wife Christine and I spend multiples of that on various insurance policies. Certainly, we defy how God spoke through his prophet Isaiah long ago: "My people, I Am your security."

Cabin as Nesting and Well-being

*"If the cabin could speak, it would say that there must be
some place in life from which to look abroad in tranquility,
in confidence, and in faith." —Walter Collins O'Kane*

Late in his life, Gaston Bachelard (1884–1962), the French philosopher and historian of science, wrote several books that explore the meanings of the elements fire, water, and air. Bachelard's method, called phenomenology, was to study direct perceptual experience. He merged the discourses of science, psychoanalysis, and aesthetics. For his materials he chose what poets had written of the elements. Mining this same vein, Bachelard wrote *The Poetics of Space*. In it he explores the meanings of the domestic spaces in our lives, the house, its interior spaces, and outer context. What did poets write about closets, cellars, garrets, stairways, roundness, even?

Bachelard's phenomenology posits that the nest is our consciousness of well-being, what makes us compare even "our homes, where there is light," with "animals in their shelter." Nests include various refuges. He quotes a painter: "The well-being I feel, seated in front of my fire, while bad weather rages out-of-doors, is entirely animal. A rat in its hole, a rabbit in its burrow, cows in the stable, must all feel the same contentment that I feel."

"Physically, the creature endowed with a sense of refuge huddles up to itself, takes to cover, hides away, lies snug, concealed," Bachelard writes. Remember finding a bird's nest as a child? "This wonder is lasting," he suggests, "and today when we discover a nest it takes us back to our childhood or, rather, to a childhood; to the childhoods we should have had. For not many of us have been endowed by life with the full measure of its cosmic implications."

For a bird a tree can be its Mateskared, as we call our family cabin in the Adirondacks. For a migrating bird, a summer tree in the northern hemisphere can be its Mateskared. Tree as refuge; tree as summer home. Henry David Thoreau tells of a woodpecker that adopted a tree in its entirety as its home. Thoreau compares the woodpecker's taking possession with a family's joy as it comes back to live in a house it long since left behind. Just so does our family —much extended now by generations—take joy in our annual summer visits to Mateskared.

"A tree becomes a nest the moment a great dreamer hides in it." Bachelard wrote. He quotes French writer and diplomat Chateaubriand: "I had set up my headquarters, like a nest, in one of these willows, and there, isolated between heaven and earth, I spent hours among the warblers." For Bachelard the "nest-house" becomes "the natural habitat of the function of inhabiting. For not only do we *come back* to it, but we dream of coming back to it . . . This sign of *return* marks an infinite number of daydreams." This dream of return "combats all absence."

One afternoon in the 1970s, my wife Christine Duewel and I were sitting by Mateskared's picture window and talking about the phenomenon of astral projection. As we elaborated on the idea, Esther, the older of my two sisters, at length piped in with: "Sometimes I just close my eyes and relax and come up here and go through the cabin and see what Mom is doing." Esther had never heard of astral projection, but she was describing it. Her combined revery and act of return testify to Bachelard's scheme. Mateskared as nest: the simplicity of its security, now also a continuity. Mateskared as "the natural habitat of the function of inhabiting." "This sign of return . . . dream of return" that "combats all absence."

Being, counsels Bachelard, begins in well-being.

Our cabin's fieldstone foundation walls its dirt-floor cellar. When I was very young the cellar was a dungeon-like unseen presence lurking beneath us.

"Don't step too far back in the pantry, Edward," my mother would say, "or you might fall into the cellar."

The cellar's reality for me came couched in that admonition. Decades later, I became enamored of the meanings of domestic spaces explored by Bachelard and learned about the dynamics of the "Shadow self" in Jungian psychology.

Certainly no precociousness was required to project psychic content on the irregularly dirt-floored and always dark, dank, root cellar. We only entered it by stooping though a very low, crude door at the front of the cabin—or via the foreboding back of the pantry, down the rickety, narrow-stepped, open stairway.

In the late 1950s, my mother Alice finally commissioned our carpenter neighbor down the road, Ernie Hitchcock, to floor over the pantry stair opening with thick plywood. My mother was not projecting her Shadow self. She was simply tired of worrying that omnipresent night noises in the cabin kitchen might mean a raccoon had gotten in through the root cellar.

"Howard! What's that noise in the kitchen?"

Her loudly whispered question to my father from their downstairs bedroom many times cut into the pitch dark, timeless chasm of my childhood cabin nights. Nor were her fears unfounded. Rats had abandoned our no-longer farm, but raccoons are often about.

The cabin's builders Pansy and Harold Allen would have stored mostly potatoes in the cellar, perhaps root crops from their kitchen garden, and no doubt some apples. The French name for potato literally means "apple of the Earth," *pomme de terre*. The analogy acknowledges that apples, which came from Central Asia, preceded potatoes in Europe. Now, if you want your potatoes French-fried, drop the *Earth*. In France our French fries are literally "fried apples," *pommes frites.*

Indeed, the potato originated in Peru in South America, and the apple came to America from Europe. These were among the happy outcomes of the great Columbian Exchange—Christopher Columbus bumping into some islands off the coast of the Americas. As agriculture increases in latitude, altitude, or both, potatoes are likely to loom large in the crop picture. Even into the 1950s locally here, Adirondack mountain farmers might begin spring with diets based on last year's potatoes and this year's early peas.

The John Dalaba family grew potatoes in the field next to ours, a field laboriously cleared of the stones and rocks that one, or several, or a team of horses could move, no doubt over many years. The potatoes seemed analogous rocks, *les roches de la terre,* to be dug out in perpetuity, as though frost-heaving yearly surfaced the new crop—locavore and the luck of the Irish.

Mateskared sits at 2,100 feet of elevation, its front windows looking out across to distant Crane Mountain, whose summit tops out at 3,254 feet above sea level. A tabloid displayed in the nearby town of North Creek's supermarket once advised: "Sea level rising 150 feet." We would be safe here—just as long as we required nothing of New York, Boston, Los Angeles, Seattle, the whole of South Florida, or much of Washington, D.C. All or most of such places would be—perhaps will be—beneath rising sea levels.

The highest point of the road that crosses Everglades National Park is just eight feet above sea level. Were the Everglades a mountain, that would be its summit.

Gardening-wise, because our cabin is pitched on the hill slope of a low mountain, we have the advantage of a generally longer frost-free growing season than Bakers Mills in the valley two miles below. Mountains generate their own air movement, a phenomenon known as orographic winds. Warm air currents rise up in the morning and cooler air passes down in the evening.

When you hear of "frost pockets," you are getting report of cold down-drafts' frosty presence. When Paul Schaefer's daughter Evelyn and her husband Don Greene gardened at the old Putnam Farm at the base of Crane Mountain, they yearly hazarded this frosty mountain-weather effect. One summer, for example they reported a maximum of 21 frost-free growing days between killing frosts. That's fine if all you want to grow and eat are peas and radishes—or perhaps the staple potatoes, which Ev and Don did not grow back then.

The fact that other hardscrabble subsistence farms once stood farther above us here on Edwards Hill, boggles the mind. I asked the late Reverend Daisy Dalaba Allen about them. Daisy was Pansy's sister and married to Earl, who was Pansy's husband Harold's cousin. Earl made maple syrup. I was down at their place for a visit and to pick up our post-vacation, over-wintering syrup ration.

Daisy recalled at least three more farms above Mateskared but said they would have been gone by 1939, when her sister Pansy and husband Harold began building their home we now call Mateskared.

When I was a young teenager, a man with the roads commission came up our hill on a tractor mounted with a sickle bar. He said he was a Hitchcock and talked of a relative once farming above us, up the road. The road as a road now ends at Mateskared but once continued straight up beside our cabin for about 400 feet. It then made a right angle turn toward Sodom, New York. Mr. Hitchcock told me his folks carried their drinking water uphill from our spring—no mean feat. A gallon of water weighs more than 8 pounds, and you wouldn't trek down that hill for just one gallon.

Daisy recalled that the road once continued beyond Chatiemac eastward to Barton Mines, the former garnet mines on the far side of our near back neighbor Gore Mountain. (At Barton Mines, someone had at last found economic sustenance from Adirondack rocks. Local garnet is still in demand for industrial abrasives.) When Daisy said that, I seemed to recall having seen an early 1930s topographical map that showed the old road going through to the hamlet of Sodom. Sodom is now a crossroads with a small, cut stone former schoolhouse near where Peaceful Valley Road splits off Route 8 about halfway between Bakers Mills and Johnsburg. Daisy's husband Earl countered that he doubted the road ever went on to Sodom.

As it turns out, Earl Allen was wrong, a rare occurrence in my experience. Recently, cartographer Tom Patterson pointed me to a US Geological Survey website of old topographical maps. Indeed, an 1898 Thirteenth Lake Quadrangle map shows the old road going through to Sodom. It also shows that today's Chatiemac Road to Chatiemac Lake did not exist then.

I can locate two former home sites above Mateskared. One stood just above where Edwards Hill Road makes its right-angle turn toward Sodom. Another, evidently much smaller place, stood a half mile or so east of the road's turn. The former used to be clearly marked by its huge lilac bushes. The latter was evidenced by a shallow cellar dent and a few less-than-random rock placements. I could imagine the dwellings but not their inhabitants' drawing sufficient sustenance from these thin soils.

When she was 13 years old, my sister Esther's daughter Layla Knox wrote the following essay as a school assignment.

"Cabin in the Mountains"
By Layla Knox*

    Our cabin in the mountains is a place for our family to get together without putting burdens on any one member. It's a time to get away from everyday hassles and to return to an unmodernized way of life. We have a cabin, woodshed and outside washstand. With chores like getting water, collecting firewood, gathering hay, not to mention cleaning out the john, there is plenty to do besides relaxing. Splitting up the chores and having to depend on everyone makes for a feeling of dependency and makes you realize everyone's need for each other.
    When the time for relaxing finally does come that's one thing we all do very well! Waking up to the smell of blueberry pancakes is what I like! Grandma likes to have her morning cup of coffee while sitting on the porch overlooking the view of Crane Mountain with the morning haze wrapped in ringlets around it, and the close and comforting look of Eleventh Mountain on the right. Slowly people awaken and everyone is gathered on the porch. Sitting in their favorite chairs the plans for the day are discussed. Maybe we'll take a hike, or a swim or maybe just a trip into town for needed supplies."

* Ed's niece

Howard Zahniser

Celestial Burial and Other Cabin Chores

*"It is the irruption of the sacred into the world,
an irruption narrated in the myths,
that establishes the world as a reality." — Mircea Eliade*

In mountainous Tibet, celestial burial is practiced. The deceased's flesh-body is cut into pieces small enough to be fed to the gathered vultures, who, because of this ritual practice, are sacred birds. Wood is too precious for funeral pyres. Soil is too scant for burials. In our part of the Adirondacks, we see few vultures, but, in part, a like ubiquity of rocks informs certain practices here.

During our early family summers on the edge of Adirondack wilderness, we children dreaded being assigned to bury the garbage, the local practice then. Waste disposal was still decentralized here in the early 1950s. To find where you might dig a hole deep enough to inter garbage was a serial ordeal of trial holes frustrated by repeat encounters with non-negotiable rocks.

I was fourteen years old the last year we buried the garbage here. My friend Larry Strausbaugh came up to the cabin with my parents and me. Given the choice of cleaning the privy—more on that and rocks later—or burying the garbage, Larry leaped to choose garbage detail. I knew I could whip through—however unpleasant a chore—"cleaning the john" in 30 minutes. By contrast, Larry might still be poking the spade then at trial holes deep enough to bury garbage.

Celestial garbage disposal would make more sense. But instead of vultures we would attract black bears. You would need an earnest backhoe to bury garbage so deeply that an opportunistic black bear couldn't get at it. Today, garbage disposal and recycling entail complex rituals—pre-printed labels, bag fees, and a full-time overseer at the landfill 10 miles' drive from our cabin.

As community service ritual, cleaning the John approaches celestial burial. Even the redoubtable Ralph Waldo Emerson asked: "What of the divine in a barber's shop or a privy?" Like celestial burial, our method of cleaning the John is grounded in ecological determinism. If you can't even bury camp garbage, how could you dig a pit toilet?

We use the "hay ball roll method." There is no pit. The first to arrive at the cabin lays down dry hay inside the John and out its open back as a 12-foot-long carpet. After you use the John, you sprinkle a partial cup of wood ashes on the pile and apply a handful of hay as covering. When the two-holer gets full-ish, more ashes and hay are applied. You then rake the accumulated hay mass out the back, rolling it up in its hay carpet to compost.

At a 25th anniversary of The Wilderness Act at our cabin, the late ecologist Anne La Bastille, author of the *Woodswoman* series of books, told my mother ours was the sweetest-smelling outhouse she'd ever encountered. Large red raspberries fruit down just downhill from the john, but we counsel guests and young children against eating them raw.

Celestial burial or hay ball roll outhouse: the point is both rocks and a dichotomy. Some Adirondack rock ranks among Earth's oldest exposed rock, but the landscape may be even newer than Tibet's great Himalayan upthrust. The late Pleistocene unpleasantness, the Ice Ages, withdrew here fewer than 10,000 years ago. (Some who winter here say it has yet to withdraw, despite present climate change.) A surge of global cooling as recently as the 1700s caused starvation in Switzerland. At Glacier Bay, Alaska then, huge developing ice sheets drove coastal Tlingit Indians from their ancestral valley homelands then and created—gouged out—magnificent Glacier Bay. The Pleistocene Ice Ages' legacy, even in the south-central Adirondacks, is the thin topsoil. Rocks and prodigious sand masses abound. Given the raw materials, stone foundations were the norm for buildings.

"Where the wilderness begins," proclaimed Paul Schaefer's August 1946 telegram that announced the completion of my parents' purchase of the cabin. Mateskared is now the last place at the end of a two-mile road out of Bakers Mills.

Were that the account of one of my grandfathers, neither of whom lived to see our place, the telegram might have read: "Ours is the *fourth* from last place above Edwards Hill Road, which, just uphill, makes a right-angle turn toward the Chatiemac Road." Years before, at least three other subsistence farms pushed against the wilderness just uphill of our place and ". . . these rough untillable acres" of Paul Schaefer's eloquent telegram.

Even into the early 1950s, the Dalaba family ran their cows on our place, fencing-in our cabin to keep their cows out. Bovine fence breaches were common, however. On our arrival at the cabin back then, we kids' first chore was to pick up the cow pies inside the barbed-wire fencing. Old pies were no sweat. Fresher ones were great temptations—for flinging at siblings. There is no running water at Mateskared. The nearest swimming holes are not within walking distance. Cow pies could become brief accretions of personal and perhaps family history.

Celestial burial practices would not have developed in the Adirondacks. Abundant trees would make ample funeral pyres. It is a constant fight now, even with resort to chain saws, to keep some of our once grazed-to-the-nubbin subsistence farm free of trees to enhance summer sojourns' moments in the Sun.

My wife Christine and I live in the Potomac River town of Shepherdstown, the next town upriver from Harpers Ferry, West Virginia. At our church there on one communion Sunday, I was contemplating the parable in the Gospel of Luke about the wise man who built his house on a rock. This parable was later co-opted as the children's example-story the "Three Little Pigs" and the wicked wolf who huffed and puffed until he blew down all but the third little pig's brick house.

The third little pig was evidently a theological Calvinist devoted to the work ethic. While taking communion, I was struck—for some reason or unreason—with how Tibetan celestial burial shared the ecological imperative of Adirondack rocks that drives Mateskared outhouse methodology.

Christine and I lived at Mateskared from late April into October the year I was discharged from the Army. I set right in to establishing a small garden. Preparing it from sod on the small flat above the cabin was one of the most laborious, tediously methodical projects I ever undertook.

"Did you have a garden that summer?" people would later ask.

"Yes, I *built* one."

Removing rocks, or at least the rocks I *could* remove, proved the easy part. I had to leave one tip of a rock where its probable boulder placed it – the farther I dug down around it, the larger the rock seemed to become, as though in some sorcerer's apprentice nightmare it actually grew in response to my attempts to remove it. I could not dig down to any point where the mass seemed to begin to lessen rather than simply to spread below me.

Perhaps our luck with that garden came because it perched *atop* a pyramid, although the efficacy of pyramids supposedly relates to focusing energy *within* them. Even such convoluted thoughts provided scant entertainment as I built the garden. I was not shaving that summer, so I didn't test this evidently pyramidal rock's ability to keep razor blades sharp.

To enlarge the garden at its east end, I carried buckets of loose soil scrounged from the nearby woods and in and around the barn. At that end of the garden, the ground fell off below a rock larger than a hassock footrest. Getting all the dirt out of the root masses of the turf clumps seemed as tough as separating out cotton seeds by hand must have been. The topsoil was far too precious for the compost pile. To garden was to unearth the Ice Age. Pulling back the topsoil's thin veneer of shallow geological time, you met the unfathomed bed of sand deposited by the great, grinding ice masses.

By May 15, striking the sod with the spade unleashed swarms of blackflies. Their pestiferousness made me wish for a return of the Ice Age—much like gardeners suffering early fall burn-out must surreptitiously pray for a killing frost. Acadians have the best name for blackflies: *bruleurs,* "burners." Christine fashioned head nets for us to fit on our brimmed hats, using old curtain material. They worked fine except that, because the curtain fabric was white and reflective, at certain angles to sunlight they blinded us. Commercial head nets are a drab, dark green on purpose.

Not long after this blackfly-besieged garden-building episode, I learned the saying of certain Zen monastics: "Nothing to do but to sit and to sweep the garden." The verb *to sit* stands for sitting meditation, their focal practice discipline. All other aspects of maintaining life are "sweeping the garden." When the poet Gary Snyder studied Zen at a monastery in Kyoto, Japan, he brought his Oregon small-farm, Mr. Fix-it gospel of efficiency to monastery chores. The other monks politely acknowledged his suggestions for efficiencies but never adopted a single one. Finally, in frustration, Snyder asked "why not?"

"All we have to do is to sit and to sweep the garden," a fellow monk explained to Snyder. "If we get better at sweeping the garden, we'll have to spend more time meditating."

In deference to faster garden-building at Mateskared, I would gladly have spent more time sitting.

Honeymoon Delayed but Prolonged

to be there, there
and blessed
—Paul Blackburn

Chris and I honeymooned at Mateskared for nearly five months, from late April through our second wedding anniversary in July, to early October. That leisurely pace contrasted starkly with our wedding weekend scenario. This was nesting versus a near one-night stand. We were married on a Saturday, and I had KP at Fort George G. Meade, Maryland early Monday morning. Monday dinner was spaghetti night. Our First Army headquarters mess hall served a few hundred troops. Spaghetti required changing the rinse water every few minutes. Otherwise, it quickly aped a reddish, coagulant sludge. Its superb coverage qualities out-classed high-grade deck paint. In retrospect, rather than griping, we should have applied for a patent. The rinse sink looked like a Superfund cleanup site.

Our wedding was a small affair in the Fellowship Hall of the Riverdale Presbyterian Church, in which I had been baptized ten years earlier. (Infant baptism is an option, not a requirement, among Presbyterians.) Twelve people attended our wedding, including Christine's father Wesley Duewel, who performed the ceremony. Christine and I have often since bragged that the soloist for President Ronald Reagan's inaugurations sang for our wedding as well. At that time though our friend Michael Ryan was then soloist and emcee for the United States Marine Corps Band.

When we wed, Michael was in the Army chorus. The macho Marine Corps later made Mike, by then quite bald, wear a wig. For our wedding, we had not! All but four of our wedding guests had logged time at Mateskared with me or I with them. This was not a pre-requisite. But, all forms of bliss should be shared.

Our extended Mateskared honeymoon was fortuitous for Christine and me. We were all but mail-order bride and bridegroom. I was then about one-quarter through my two years as an Army draftee during Viet Nam. My last nine months of service would be spent in South Korea.

Chris and I had courted mostly by mail after her brother John introduced us via that medium. I went to college with John. He would show me pictures of his kid sister, who attended the University of Wisconsin, Madison. On the backs of the photos, John wrote physical statistics that were supposed to impress me. Unfortunately, I didn't know enough to be impressed, except that I *knew* I was supposed to be. Nor, do I think, John knew. We were enrolled in a repressive evangelical college surrounded by western Illinois cornfields. Students had to sign a pledge against drinking, smoking, dancing, and going to the movies—even during Christmas, Easter, and summer vacations. Ironically, many students watched all the television they wanted.

The only reason our college pledge forms did not mention sex was that the administration feared that some students might ask what that was. It helps contain a student body socially if many students think that kissing, for example, causes pregnancy. The marriage-and-family course the college had finally gotten up the nerve to offer—this was the mid-1960s—was strictly a lecture course, not a lab course.

Most advantageous for me, as relatively new spouse at Mateskared, was that Christine could see me there in the world's one place in which I most knew the routines of daily subsistence. This included cooking. At the cabin, I also felt most competent at what 1960s philosophy textbooks called "being-in-the-world." I even knew how to—metaphorically, at least—"flush the toilet," which stood outside and just downhill to your right.

I don't know what Christine then perceived as of particular advantage for her at Mateskared. I do know I was in heaven, which is most convincing with your Beatrice by your side.

For the first couple months, it was too cold to raise bread dough inside the cabin. In the drafty cabin we could not get or sustain an optimal yeast-action temperature via the open fire. The lowest setting on our electric skillet was too high. We finally hit on parking our 1965 Corvair, that amazingly trusty Nader-mobile, in full sunlight and regulating its interior temperature by adjusting the windows. Our method might have disgusted whoever wrote our *Uncle John's Bread Book,* but it sure pleased the yeast.

By then, we'd already been married long enough to ascertain that neither of us really liked to cook day in and day out. Christine had grown up in India in boarding school or at home with a cook. I had learned most of what I knew about cooking visually, by hanging around my mother's kitchen activities. I knew what stuff was supposed to end up looking like. I didn't always know how you got to that end point. I was most adept at camping cookery.

That Mateskared was neighbor to genuine wilderness was not entirely new to Christine that year of belated honeymooning. My obligatory break between Army basic training and reporting to my duty station at Fort Meade two years earlier had coincided with her spring break at the University of Wisconsin. We capitalized on that cosmic coincidence by venturing to Mateskared. Once there we backpacked from the cabin the three and a half miles back to Bog Meadow for an overnight. It was mid-April. We were lucky our pup tent wasn't crushed by snow. We were lucky we didn't freeze. The Force was with us for this precious, non-postal time together.

To know that wilderness is your neighbor is one thing. To have *wilderness* pronounced in warm-breathed gutturals by a black bear brings it up "close and personal." In 1975, Christine and I both had quit our jobs in Washington, D.C. and spent from late April to early October at Mateskared. Before other family began to arrive for their summer vacations, we slept in the upstairs bedroom over the kitchen and living room.

One night, Christine was awakened from deep sleep by the insistent voice of a friend from our meditation group—who lived five hundred miles from Mateskared—calling her name. Christine got out of bed and peered out our upstairs bedroom window. As soon as she got her head out the window and looked down, a black bear below looked up and growled sharply. Christine flung herself back from the window with such force that she managed to wake me up.

Before my siblings and I went forth and multiplied, yea, even unto two additional generations' worth, my mother, Alice, used to get to spend the odd week or so by herself in late July or early August at Mateskared. One night during such cabin solitude, she heard a noise in the yard area beside the kitchen and living room. She walked up to the side window to look out. When she got close enough to the window that no reflected light inside the cabin blocked her view, she realized a bear was nosing the other side of the window pane.

Another "neighbor" to reckon with!

Cabin Yard: The Acting Rock and 'Steamboat Rock'

Gray-green lichens slowly increase their hegemony on the large rock that sits below Mateskared and fifteen feet west of its outhouse. My niece Layla Ward remembers sitting on this rock as a child and fearing falling off. Its steep downhill side slopes into depths of tall blackberry plants, ferns, goldenrod, and fireweed.

I was down in those tall plants some years ago to fetch a stray Frisbee for Christine and our younger son, Eric. Even as an adult, I experience some anxiety in the dense, cloaking foliage. Plant tips can reach my neck. I feel like Snoopy in the "Peanuts" cartoon, caught in tall grass. The rock's uphill side and an old driveway pull-in from the road define a mowing line for the cabin yard. The interface of mowed and not mowed creates an ecotone, an edge between yard culture and the beginnings of wild nature's recovery to its former forest estate. We struggle to deny the trees a foothold too near the outhouse or the cabin, even.

A Mateskared photo from around 1950 shows our mother Alice walking up toward the cabin through this downhill pasture. What has today been re-taken—where allowed to farther downhill—as young forest of forty- to fifty-foot-tall trees, shows in the photograph as bare pasture. It was grazed to the nubbin then by John and Hester Dalaba's cows—and punctuated by ubiquitous immovable rocks. Vegetation now obscures all but this one great rock.

"Karen used to get up on that rock and do acting," my mother remarked. She was remembering the rock just as I did. My sister Karen adopted the rock as her stage. She would cajole us, even as teenagers or older, into taking turns climbing to its summit to speechify or to declaim.

The Acting Rock became even more effective after we added a front porch to the cabin in 1967, although by then my generation was already through college. The declaimer's audience could now be more cohesive and comfortably seated on the roofed porch.

I credit the Acting Rock with Karen's mid-life career switch to becoming an Episcopal priest. That I identify the Acting Rock with speechifying—its nearly square-foot summit flatness doesn't quite parallel the ground—may betray my narrow concept of acting as delivering soliloquies! Nor am I sure what it says about my concept of the priesthood. My brother Mathias is an ordained minister, too. But, with a PhD. in Arabic, he taught university and college comparative religion and cross-cultural courses, and tutored Arabic. In retirement, he still writes international scholarly material about the Koran.

The photo features "The Acting Rock" on which the Zahniser kids used to stand to speechify folks on the cabin porch. Mathias "Matt Zahniser and the late Karen Z. Bettacchi, went on to become ordained ministers. The Acting Rock also suggests the structure of "Steamboat Rock" in the Green River in Echo Park National Monument, Utah. The fight against a proposed dam on the Green, that would have inundated much of Steamboat Rock, was a conservation battle, led by Howard Zahniser of The Wilderness Society and David R. Brower of The Sierra Club, which was to lauch the campaign for what became the National Wilderness System Act of Congress, which now protects 111 million acres of federal wilderness areas.

Echo Park, Prelude to the 1964 U.S. Wilderness Act

One August morning as Mom and I sat on the cabin porch drinking coffee and staring at "The View," aka Crane Mountain, I was struck by how much the Acting Rock looks like a much scaled-down version of Steamboat Rock. Steamboat Rock looms massive inside a looping bend in the Green River in the Pat's Hole or Echo Park area of Dinosaur National Monument in Utah.

No mere rock, it's a massive, high, sheer peninsula set in its great looping river meander. In the 1950s, it would come to symbolize permanent protection of nature in the struggle over the proposed Echo Park Dam. The U.S. Bureau of Reclamation planned to dam the Green River just downstream. Most of Steamboat Rock would have been submerged and Pat's Hole or Echo Park obliterated. So would much of the Yampa River tributary that joins the Green River upstream. One of the points conservations made with Congress was that if part of the National Park System was vulnerable to such a dam proposal, then no category of federal land was permanently protected.

Steamboat Rock takes its name from how the motion of the great Green River, a major Colorado River tributary, makes it appear as though the rock were chugging along through the waterway. Our whole family was to see Steamboat Rock in 1953 from down in Pats Hole. ("Hole" is a western U.S. term for a mountain-encircled valley.) Seen from on or across the river, Steamboat Rock looks like a great, archetypal *Mississippi Queen* triple-decker stern-wheeler putting its shoulder to the Green River's heady current.

It is fair to say that upon Steamboat Rock today's 111-million-acre National Wilderness Preservation System would one day be founded.

It is likewise fair to say that, had Paul Schaefer not lured my father Howard Zahniser to the Adirondacks in 1946 to fight dam threats to Forest Preserve wildlands here, the rag-tag band of conservationists would not have achieved saving Utah's Steamboat Rock and much of Dinosaur National Monument from being inundated behind a U.S. Bureau of Reclamation dam.

That utterly surprising victory in Utah came against politically powerful and well-funded western water interests, their national legislators, and the federal bureaucracies supposedly regulating rivers. The conservationists' victory emboldened my father and David Brower, then head of the Sierra Club, to turn their national anti-dam coalition to the pursuit of federal legislation to protect wilderness on vast reaches of federal public lands.

Environmental historian Roderick Nash characterized the defeat of Echo Park Dam as a "decision for permanence." The final settlement my father negotiated on behalf of the conservationists at last held National Park System lands to be inviolable.

This first great national grass-roots conservation victory also redeemed the 1913 vote by Congress to allow the magnificent Hetch Hetchy Valley— inside Yosemite National Park—to be dammed and flooded. Losing Hetch Hetchy was the most profound disappointment in the conservation career of Sierra Club founder John Muir.

Proof of my speculation about the Adirondack influence in the Echo Park fight, if there is proof, no doubt resides in the personal papers and Adirondack conservation collection of the late Paul Schaefer. Paul penned the elegant telegram text now burned into Mateskared's fireplace mantel in my father's block-lettering handscript.

One direct connection—to the proverbial bottom line—is well documented. The Echo Park fight cost far more money than small membership organizations like The Wilderness Society and Sierra Club routinely wrangled in the 1950s. Defense of the environment did not become a groundswell movement until 1970 and after.

Zahnie first met the man who would bankroll crucial points in the Echo Park campaign while he and Paul Schaefer were fighting the Adirondack dams in the 1940s and early 1950s. Environmental historian Roderick Nash has written that "In the course of defending the Adirondacks in the 1940s, Howard Zahniser became acquainted with the wealthy St. Louis chemical manufacturer and Sierra Club member Edward C. Mallinckrodt, Jr. When the defense of Dinosaur moved into the conservation spotlight, Zahniser persuaded him to become its patron."

On many of my father's work trips to the West in the 1950s he would stop in St. Louis. There he would brief "Mr. Mallinckrodt,"—as he spoke of him to us children—or ask him for money. He was visibly impressed with Mr. Mallinckrodt's formal manner and attitude toward his wealth and the needs of conservation. Zahnie would adopt his manner to illustrate his generosity. "You tell me what the need is," Mr. Mallinckrodt would say, "and I will just kiss"—and here my father would mimic Mr. Mallinckrodt's gesture of kissing the gathered thumb and fingertips of his hand to broadcast his money to the wind—"the money goodbye!"

Broadcast mostly to printing companies, newspaper advocacy ads, and U.S. post offices, the money did the job. Conservationists foiled the politically powerful western hydropower lobby. It was the 1940s western Adirondack Black Water Wars redux. My father negotiated the Dinosaur settlement for the conservationists. The resulting legislation was signed by President Dwight David Eisenhower, who gave my father a pen he used to sign the Act of Congress.

The projected Echo Park Dam was already being engineered, and its water and evaporation dynamics had been developed, when Zahnie and David Brower started advocating stopping it. This was reminiscent of the Black River Wars, in which the dams were already engineered, and Paul Schaefer and Zahnie were told it was "a lost cause." Here again, Zahnie and The Wilderness Society and David Brower and the Sierra Club built a constituency, national this time, to fight another lost cause. Again, they won.

My all-time favorite quotation about my father came from his close friend and associate Olaus J, Murie, longtime head of The Wilderness Society Governing Council. Murie once said "Zahnie has unusual tenacity in lost causes." That was a skill he learned in New York State from and with Paul Schaefer as they fought the dams proposed for the western Adirondacks. Unusual tenacity in lost causes. Think of 66 drafts of wilderness bills and 19 public hearings nationwide over eight years of struggle. The cause was wilderness preservation, which merely called into question the Great American Idea of Progress.

This is an attitude of humility, to recognize that we do not know enough to manipulate the natural world, the more than human world of nature, without possibly untoward results. In 1955, Zahnie gave a speech preparatory to the introduction of the first wilderness bill in the U.S. Congress. "It is characteristic of wilderness to impress its visitors with their relationship to other forms of life," Zahnie said. "In the wilderness it is thus possible to sense most keenly our human membership in the whole community of life on the Earth. And in this possibility is perhaps one explanation for our modern deep-seated need for wilderness."

At Mateskared, these feelings are palpable. My father took inspiration from them for his thinking about wilderness and our human relation to it. Here the forest relentlessly overtakes former subsistence farmland. A feeling persists here, which Aldo Leopold articulated, that wilderness is the raw material out of which we have hammered this artifact called civilization. Historic Iroquois or Mohawk Indigenous peoples would no doubt have found Leopold's statement realistic and not hyperbolic. As Rachel Carson took pains to point out, it is far more important—particularly for human *and* Earth futures—to *feel* this stake than to know it. That an old school district exists in the Siamese Ponds Wilderness seems now like a fragment from far historic time.

From Yard Rocks to Big Rock

Under the big maple tree above the northwest corner of our barn at Mateskared, a large rock holds a mixed history for me. It's a rounded-off triangular solid. As kids, my three siblings and I slid down it, putting the seats of our pants at risk. A rounded pocket two-thirds down its topmost, steeper slope transformed the rock as our stone throne.

Part of my memory of this rock is based on a photograph and is false. I recalled a snapshot of my father (Howard Zahniser) and me on the rock about 1950. I wear a beanie cap. But later finding the photo, I discovered we are on a different rock, farther uphill, now hidden in recovering pasture.

A visceral memory records an accident when I was six years old. Standing on the rock's lower, gentler slope, I hold a cast-off, wood-handled fishing rod I found in the woodshed. As I fling the rod off the rock, a long sliver of its wooden handle sticks in my hand. I vividly recall how quickly the heady feeling of flinging the rod became the pain of splinter. My mother worked the splinter out from under my skin with a sterilized needle. That no one else still holds this traumatic memory—founded on a rock—might call it into question.

That misremembered 1950 rock-top photo of my father and me gained strength when I first sat my son Justin atop the stone throne rock. Over the years, both he and our younger son Eric mastered its domain. Our three generations—with our sons' Justin's and Eric's two children each now—have had no discernible material impact on this rock. But I take it on faith that the lichens etch the rock to buttress our thin Adirondack soil. For my old garden plot's sake, I wish they'd hurry up.

Memory is a grab-bag. Other people may not share your version. My late mother Alice had correctly remembered that the 1950 photo featured the rock farther uphill. I later found the photo and included it in the book of my father's Adirondack writings *Where Wilderness Preservation Began*. Sometimes, place is space that—like the deceased—evokes multiple memories and multiple histories.

My mother Alice lived the last 20 years of her life in a retirement community in Chambersburg, Pennsylvania. Mennohaven is run by warm-spirited Mennonites. It exemplifies the Biblical "daily bread" economy, which a parable in *The Gospel of Luke* favors in contrast to our culture's prevailing "storehouse economy." Excess productive energy is best stored as goodwill in family and neighbors as everyone's daily bread. Wealth implies excessive barns or warehouses as private hoards. *Mea culpa.*

Not long after my father died, my mother turned in her settler's card and, by stages, renewed her migrant's card. (She would survive my father by 50 years.) Since the demolition of my childhood home—then her life's longest home—my mother moved seven times. The net effect vested her sense of extended-family homeness in Mateskared. When she moved from her apartment in West Virginia to Mennohaven, my wife Christine and I said she was just moving an hour closer to the Adirondacks.

Our extended family now gathers at Mateskared. Every few years, my mother's grandchildren used to hold a workweek they called "Cousins Week." When our sons Justin and Eric were the only cousin minors, Christine and I justified joining those gatherings. One August week seventeen of us centered on the cabin for clearing brush and trees, repainting the porch deck and outdoor furniture, patching the outhouse roof, clearing out gobs of wet maple leaves around the barn's uphill wall, and cooking quasi-institutional meals for the gaggle of relations.

Big Rock

Mateskared yard rocks would look like mere stones if plunked down next to Big Rock. It is useless but true to tell someone "Big Rock is as big as our barn." Best to walk them to the thing itself. Our barn is smallish, its attached cowshed like a half garage. Big Rock similarly sits in recent-growth forest of recovering pasture land, perhaps a mile east of, and downhill from, Mateskared.

Big Rock is a glacial erratic boulder. It would have been rafted to its spot by a glacier and then abandoned when the glacier melted back in retreat. "Erratic" means that Big Rock's composition likely has little relation to the rocks around it. That's certainly true for scale, making Big Rock surprising, even when you know what you are looking for. Or think you do.

Why should a rock as big as a small barn sit by itself in the woods with no rock of comparable size nearby? It begs the motive power of Ice Age ice sheets. Big Rock invokes awe, that sense of the sacred induced by the diminutive effect, of feeling your smallness amidst the cosmic order. It's what drove the architecture of Europe's great Gothic cathedrals. Big Rock is big, and scale-distorting isolation amplifies its bigness.

Paul Schaefer first told me Big Rock was a glacial erratic. The only glaciers I knew firsthand then were small mountain glaciers snugged into the Teton Range's serrated skyline over Jackson Hole, Wyoming. Teton glaciers gave no satisfactory mental image of Big Rock's glacial transport. Pleistocene ice sheets were a mile or more thick. Big Rock would ride such a conveyor belt like a mere plum.

Imagine standing next to the face of a mile-thick ice sheet. This strains the diminutive effect. For all its 3,254-foot elevation and relative isolation, Crane Mountain, which doesn't even rise from sea level, cannot begin to suggest the vastness of ice that rafted Big Rock into place.

Since farming ceased here, forest has worked overtime to cast shade on Big Rock. Before I was a teenager, we made family lunch expeditions through the Dalaba Farm and sugar bush, across the Cold Spring Brook's tiny headwaters and through mixed hardwoods to Big Rock. Improvised ladders sometimes gave access to its flat but sloping top. When I was young, "summiting" Big Rock was scary and magical. We sometimes packed a lunch to eat up on top.

And on top, what a view then—off to the southeast we thought we saw the mountains of Vermont. Why not? *Vermont* means "Green Mountains," and off to the south lie row on row of mountains that, in certain lights, do look green. In other lights you might announce: "From atop Big Rock you can see across Lake Champlain to Bluemont." Now you see nothing from atop Big Rock but the rock underfoot, some sky overhead, and into treetops that now engulf this behemoth hump of erratic elsewhere. The fecundity of forest recovery has its scenic downside.

In my mind's eye, I can still look to Vermont over sandwiches and lemonade with our family of six, perhaps Paul's wife Carolyn "Ma" Schaefer and the four Schaefer kids, and – I distinctly picture – Melvin Allen, Pansy and Harold's son, then about eleven years old.

One evening, with 90 minutes of daylight left and needing a brisk walk, I set off to measure Big Rock. I wanted to verify my second-generation likening of its mass to our small barn. The trail was still well cleared. Brush overhung only a small bit through an old clearing. In my memory that stretch of trail has been clogged with thickets since a few years after the Dalabas left their Hillmount Farm.

In open hardwoods, I heard – but didn't see – a deer bound off downhill. A bear sounds like one mad brush-crashing scramble in startled flight. Most forest sounds grow more startling with dusk, as vision grows less sure, more tricky and illusive.

Sometimes a low cairn of rocks atop a bathtub-sized rock marks the short turn-off to Big Rock. Big Rock lies about 125 feet uphill from the trail in recovering deciduous forest. At dusk, you can mistake it as more forest floor: Big Rock as back drop. But I knew what to look for. Ever larger on site than in memory, Big Rock never fails to impress. The largest nearby rock is but a wedge-shaped slab, a spalled-off chunk of its former self.

I had brought a 25-foot measuring tape. Big Rock measures 41 feet uphill. The downhill, front side measured 35 feet. Uphill it tapers to a bit lesser thickness. I judged—in basketball hoop heights—that on its downhill side the crest may sit about 23 feet above the forest floor. My inner hoop-height calculator is quite accurate.

From Big Rock, having a sufficiency of daylight left in the woods, I continued on the main trail to the power lines along Chatiemac Road. Like a monument to domesticity, the fieldstone chimney of a burned cabin stood above the cleared powerline right-of-way that was dotted with milkweed plants. I didn't linger. A sunset spread to the southeast above the far mountains once visible from Mateskared and from Big Rock. Then I hotfooted it back around Edwards Hill to the cabin.

When she talked about Big Rock, Daisy Allen would somewhere tuck in its other name, Dunlop's Rock, maintaining the human depth of its layered place-making history.

Early Morning on the Cabin Porch

the world is a flower in space
its bloom and decay are delusions
—Stonehouse

The importance of religion is not so much the forgiveness of sins as it is awareness and gratitude, I tell our sons Eric and Justin, then aged twelve and fifteen, respectively. Amazing grace throbs in daily life, I tell them. There are debts of love owed life.

We are not Jewish, but I sometimes think it would be easier for me to teach them the Hebrew language, which I do not know, than to tell them about this untellable story, which, in a way, I do know.

We are sitting on their front porch at Mateskared. I call this their front porch because Mateskared used to be my parents' cabin and now it belongs to my brother Mathias and me as surviving siblings. I could tell my sons: Look, true future ownership of this cabin resides in your gonads or those of your cousins.

But, I am not even enough of the shadow of a rabbi to broach such discourse this early in the morning.

I have already discussed sex and sexuality with them, when each was nine years old. In retrospect, that was no more difficult than taking the Graduate Record Exams—which lasted all day—using a soft, computer-readable magnetic-lead pencil and those huge, page-wide multiple-choice rows of tiny light blue vertical rectangles made up of dashed lines. By afternoon, they were dancing—not my sons, but those light-blue dashed rectangles. Maybe I could make up a multiple-choice test about religion for my kids, but should I grade it on the curve of but two or pass-fail?

Justin and Eric are up fairly early this morning. I've been up reading and writing since six o'clock. Vacation protocol is that people sleep-in as long as they like, which my wife Christine and my late mother Alice were doing as we spoke.

What about you? Would you rather sleep-in or hazard talking to your kids about religion?

What if you were just graded pass-fail?

Justin and Eric stare off into space at the view down and across the valley to Crane Mountain. Odds are—even in this deterministic world—they are making up new characters for their role-playing games. If I tried to make them read the Hebrew Scriptures, they would grouse no end. If I suggested instead that you might get great ideas for role-playing characters and scenarios out of the Hebrew Scriptures, they might fight over the chance to devour it. Motivation is key to the parental movement of children.

Christine and I do not want to burden our children with metaphysical guilt or with the notion that one should invest only in another as yet unseen world. My aging grandmothers used to sit in their rocking chairs and read their Bibles every day. This was before my family got a TV. Maybe they were just watching their Bibles. But the way my grandmothers talked about religion, you could tell they read their Bibles like they were cramming for their finals.

Our paternal grandmother once corrected my brother Matt—he was maybe 14 years old. He had just squirted himself in one eye with acrid orange-rind spray and blurted out "I hate orange peels!"

"You should never hate anything but sin," she scolded him.

That's just about my favorite story to tell therapists. Most of the therapists I've known only think of religion as something that happened to other people in the past and should now be the subject of a Twelve-Step group.

"Hi, my name is Ed, and I'm the adult child of an overly religious family system."

"Hi, Ed! Keep coming back. It works if you work it."

Earlier this morning pockets of mist still sat in the foothill valleys and other low spots leading up to the base of Crane Mountain. Seen from our porch at Mateskared, they look like ponds and lakes. Most people sleep too late to see them. These illusionary bodies of water remind me of the part in the book of the New Testament now called "To the Hebrews," where it says "we are surrounded by so great a cloud of witnesses. . ."

Justin and Eric are beginning to wake up enough to begin to externalize their energy. They won't be content to sit still on the porch much longer. It is as though their consciousness takes a certain amount of time to reorient itself and then this Psalmist-on-duty in their brain cries out "Sleepers, awake!"

This means I have just minutes left to talk with them meaningfully about religion.

Maybe I should be autobiographical and tell them "Look, before you guys were born, I spent ten years growing into an earnest meditation practice. What most people call mysticism comes down to a simple, profound gratitude. When Godself told Moses his or her name was I Am – or I will be what I will be – Godself wasn't shucking Moses. Real experience of God comes when you finally are absolutely certain that when you pray you are talking to yourself."

There is another wonderful part in "To the Hebrews" in the New Testament where it says—and will repeat it twice later—"Today, if you hear his voice, do not harden your hearts as in the rebellion."

That's what I should tell my sons: "Today, if you hear that voice, do not harden your hearts."

I wonder what Crane Mountain is thinking? It sits off by itself and towers over its near neighbors. It has one real pond on it, a small lake halfway up, which faces heaven like an unblinking third eye. I once spent time on Crane alone for an abbreviated vision quest—no fire, no cooked food. Maybe I should tell my sons "Look, what I learned up there was not to expect anything of the mountain. It just is."

Our two guys will want their breakfast now. Last night, before bedtime, I told them I'd make French toast this morning.

"Well," I tell them matter-of-factly, getting out of my porch chair, "On this day in 1600, after eight years in prison, Giordano Bruno was burned at the stake by the Inquisition for heresy. You guys still want that French toast for breakfast?"

Our Spring vs. Fossil Water

If there is magic on this planet it is contained in water.
—Loren Eiseley

Our understanding that the volume of stream flow and other surface-water phenomena directly relate to the amount of precipitation is relatively recent. It is roughly the same age as the United States. We owe this idea's formulation to a Frenchman who calculated and compared surface area and precipitation with stream flow, publishing his findings in the 1770s. Conventional wisdom had held that water simply bubbled-up from within the Earth, where—and here competing theories surely varied—it was generated.

Given the most short-range empiricism, i.e. what you see is what you get, Mateskared's setting could support both theories. The persistence and apparent equanimity of our spring do make it appear that its water might bubble up from within the Earth, that rain might be irrelevant to its sure supply. By contrast, the intermittent stream behind our barn flows as a lively freshet in late July or August only after protracted rainfall or concerted storms. Otherwise, in August the stream neither murmurs nor sings.

One summer, we were forewarned on our arrival that an extended drought was in progress. Nevertheless, our intermittent stream was to flow two times after we arrived at Mateskared on July 23. Even the stream's intermittent flowing could challenge or confuse empirical observation. Sometimes the heavy flow starts only well after the rain quits falling, thereby making this watershed discharge look like sleight of hand.

Our spring's water does not bubble up, because, below-ground— you would need Superman's x-ray vision to observe this—its water is trickling down. Only when the water nears the surface does gravity, given the weight of the water's flow above our spring's hillside setting, force it to emerge as flow. Once the water reaches pool elevation in our spring's barrel, gravity sends the excess flow downhill.

That rain and other forms of precipitation, including atmospheric moisture condensed as dew, should water our spring and intermittent stream retains an aura of magic for me. One summer in the 1960s, drought in downstate New York caused big problems for farmers. Paul Schaefer assured me that was not the case here in the Adirondacks, because of the heavy dew.

Earth's overall water supply is fixed and apparently constant, because gravity prevents water's escaping our atmosphere. From a creationist viewpoint, our hydrosphere certainly could appear to argue for design. Its elegance also suffices to seem to argue for a Hydrospheric Cosmological Principle rather than the Anthropic

Cosmological Principle. That is, Earth may have evolved to express this hydrosphere phenomenon rather than to express human beings.

At Mateskared, we are fortunate to have our drinking water supplied on this one-to-one basis, temporally speaking. Even before Harold and Pansy Allen turned our plot on Edwards Hill Road over to my parents, people have been confident in our spring's ability to mete out recent precipitation today and again tomorrow and tomorrow. In the Sahara Desert, water is lifted to the surface by modern gasoline or electric powered pumps. That water probably accumulated underground no less than 10,000 years ago, as runoff as Pleistocene Era glaciers, those sometimes mile-thick continental-scale ice sheets, melted back.

One need not venture to Africa to witness fossil-water mining. In our U.S. Southwest and Great Basin regions, pumps now mine Ice Age water stored underground in aquifers. Surely we do this with no confidence that another Ice Age will supply more water before one of two untoward events takes place. Either a particular aquifer will go bone dry, or its water level will fall too low for pumps to lift to the surface affordably. Some remaining water cannot now be pumped to the surface, because its grit content strips the pumps' valves. By contrast, at Mateskared we are blessed to drink contemporary water, not fossil water.

Ten thousand-year-old water tastes good, but the human brain and heart are 73 percent water. We therefore want confidence in a supply that suggests we merely quaff its interest, or current income at most. We do not wish to swallow our capital wholesale and draw down the principle to naught. While we may complain about two-week runs of rainy weather here, we do not want to seem ungrateful for Mateskared's unfailing spring.

My First Trout and 'The Rainmakers'

My advice to nine-year-old wanna-be trout anglers is: "Do *not* wear a sweater." Repeat: "Do *not* wear a sweater." My earliest trout fishing days in and around Bakers Mills, New York in today's Siamese Ponds Wilderness Area were frustrating because my own fishhooks invariably caught mainly my sweater. And we mostly used night crawlers not artificial flies then. Better to wear something less adept at snagging stray hooks. Try thick vinyl, maybe!

I was considered too young to carry a knife of my own. To resume fishing once I had snagged my own sweater, I had to plead with Cub Schaefer to *stop* fishing long enough to come cut my hook out. This could happen four or five times in a day's fishing. It happened around Bakers Mills, and it happened in the High Peaks. For purposes of fishing, you might as well be that fabled archetypal snake with its tail in its mouth as have your barbed fishhook fixed to your own sweater.

One of the mysteries of my youth is: Why did I always have to depend on Cub for this? It was my nearly seven years older brother Matt on whom I depended for most other aspects of life support—physical, moral, and psychic—whenever we were away from the cabin and our parents. Without Matt I would not have been allowed to *go* on the trips. Maybe Matt carried only nail clippers, for snipping leaders or snelled hooks. Matt knew that Cub, ever our equipment expert in those days, had The Knife. Matt was a fly-tying angler not above using nightcrawlers. For whatever reason, I had to wait for Cub to cut hooks out.

That was tough, too. Not that I was particularly impatient, but Cub was the most single-minded angler I've ever met east of the Mississippi River. Later, as I reached the age of declining idol worship, I realized Cub's singular focus was not so much the fishing as a gestalt but his irrepressible drive to get to the next fishing hole first. Fishing small streams for trout comes down to addressing the stream's most likely as-yet-undisturbed pools.

This is especially true when the potential for disturbance is six boys, all but one under thirteen years old. Optimal pools for trout may be some distance apart on small Adirondack streams. If you can hit all the optimal pools first, before anybody else in your group wets a worm in them . . . well, that's how you up the chance of catching your limit. And catching your limit—10 trout—was our *ne plus ultra.*

"I caught my limit." Ten trout. I never got to say that magic four-word sentence east of the Hundredth Meridian until I was 14 years old.

I was seven years old when I caught my first trout. Paul Schaefer set the whole experience up, including holding Cub at bay until I got first crack at the optimal pool. Over subsequent years and years of fishing from our base at Mateskared, I was to realize that Paul had set me up with one of the best pools in our entire topographic quadrangle, the pool at the base of Bog Meadow Falls on Round Pond Brook. Round Pond Brook drained what was to become the center of my psychic universe, the falls' namesake Bog Meadow, an intermittent beaver pond.

I was using the telescope rod Paul had sent to me for Christmas the previous winter. You can imagine my sense of anticipation—seven months' worth by August. Maybe the beaver had Bog Meadow at an unfishable water level for a seven-year-old. I don't know. But Paul didn't have me fish there. Bog Meadow is three and a half miles in from Paul's former log cabin off Edwards Hill Road out of Bakers Mills.

In those days, we picked up the trail at his cabin, which meant walking more than a half mile down the road and then back in to his cabin—none of this *toward* Bog Meadow—before we hit the trail beyond his cabin. On this, my first-trout day, we continued on the trail around the perimeter of Bog Meadow and headed down toward the Second Pond Flow. A mile or so below Bog Meadow, Paul led us bushwhacking through the woods to the waterfall.

Paul positioned me at the base of the pool and told me to cast to its head, just shy of where the falls broke the pool surface and raised their white froth that rode this water that pooled dark with tree bark tannins. I hurled my night crawler there. The line began to sink. Then it took to a steady straightening.

"Set the hook, Eddie," Paul quietly coached me.

Via the metal of a kid's first telescope fly rod, a primal communication of sheer sensitivity surged between the fighting action of my first trout and the hands and forearm of yet another scion of Izaak Walton. As I worked the trout toward shore I might as well have been the one in the water. This was a baptism, total immersion, an initiation not unlike the sprinkled one that lay five years in my future in a church.

The real hook gets set in the angler by that first trout.

This quasi-religious ritual, appropriately involves fish not symbolically but actually. Cub witnessed this in full, no doubt covetously. He still stood where Paul had placed him, looking down from atop the fifteen-foot waterfall. The instant I beached my trout, Cub unleashed his worm toward the pool's dark water. No matter: I was transfixed.

One summer, any day all six of us kids managed to go off fishing together it always, always rained. We got rained on so consistently that, as a full group, we called ourselves "The Rainmakers." If one or more of our total group couldn't go, however, it wouldn't rain. Hankering after first shot at the optimal trout pools were Cub, Matt, me, Johnny Hitchcock, Tommy Taylor, and Tommy Sennet. The two Tommy's were Schaefer family friends from Schenectady. Johnny was the son of Howard and Betty Hitchcock, who lived then in the next place below Harold and

Pansy Allen's place on Edwards Hill Road. Matt would have been 15, Johnny maybe 13, Cub and the two Tommy's 11 or so.

By summer's end, I'd had so many hooks cut out of my poor sweater I looked like a street urchin out of Charles Dickens. I probably *smelled* like an urchin from the fish markets—I did catch fish on most trips.

"Doesn't Eddie look happy this summer?"

"Yes, fishing with the older kids has done wonders for him, but it *is* a shame he can't wear nicer clothes. Just *look* at that sweater!"

When, in later years, I took our sons Justin and Eric back to these scenes of the Rainmakers' greatest piscatorial glory, I have been astounded at how small some of those streams are compared to former memories of them. The Rainmakers used to fish Cold Spring Brook down Edwards Hill Road behind Daisy and Earl Allen's former place, now their daughter Kjerstia's home.

One time, as we hiked through the tall grassy meadow of its flat, open floodplain—or perhaps former beaver meadow—Cub relocated the stream by stepping in it nearly up to his hip. Cub never saw it before he was in it. The brook was barely wider than the length of his foot, which even then suggested he would end up more than six feet tall like his father Paul.

Tall grasses flopped over to obscure the channel. But the stream was down-cut deep into turf and soil. The Rainmakers pulled five or six nice brook trout, seven to nine inches long, out of a stretch of stream so narrow only a pack of kids would bother trying to work their worms into it.

Photo, *left to right: Mathias Zahniser, Francis "Cub" Schaefer, John Hitchcock, Tommy Sennet, Tommy Taylor.*

'Gotcha One Donut!'

The Rainmakers' greatest of summer adventures left me behind at Mateskared, so technically it was not a Rainmakers' expedition. Or, so I still console myself to think. Matt led the rest of the crew backpacking to a set of recent beaver ponds on Round Pond Brook above Bog Meadow. For several days there, they had some of the best trout fishing Matt ever experienced in the eastern United States. Those beaver ponds were at just the right stage of their life cycle to be swarming with trout. On more than one day the five of them caught their limits.

The crew packed in several pounds of bacon, mainly to use its grease to cook the anticipated trout. This provisioning strategy worked probably better than they had planned because, once they were back in the wilderness, Tommy Sennet announced that he did not eat fish. But the only other protein choice was bacon, pounds of bacon. Tommy Sennet ate the bacon. The other boys ate the fish. Tommy Taylor had seen every movie released in the Schenectady area for several years. No doubt he recounted a big-screen story with a similar plot. No matter what we did that summer, Tommy Taylor could compare it one-to-one with a movie he'd seen. Rather than put the money into baby sitters, he said, his parents simply let him go to the movies. You could not one-up him on movies.

Bacon was not the *only* other food choice. Johnny Hitchcock's mom Betty had made up five dozen donuts, one dozen per camper, for the trip. As often happens—because backpacking groups become subcultures by the second or third day out—the donuts quickly transcended mere food status and became objects of barter. They were tickets out of a disliked camp chore. They were tokens of payment for breaches of the subcultural penal code: "Gotcha one donut!" If the group backed up the witness for the prosecution, you paid the claimant one donut.

In some cases you could protect yourself from penalty for a verbal breach of the behavioral code by interjecting "Don't got me!" before anyone else could blurt "Gotcha one donut!"

No doubt those trip days were not among the quietest few days ever witnessed by otherwise placid beaver ponds in what is now the Siamese Ponds Wilderness. My brother Matt later earned advanced degrees in theology and comparative religion, and a Ph.D. in Arabic from the Johns Hopkins University. I have not run the following by him, but I suspect his role as subadult-in-charge of four younger teens on this backpack fishing trip taught him both the skills and peculiar quality of patience that a career of various teaching positions must surely demand.

Cub Schaefer and the Bull

Adirondack summers for the Zahniser clan on Edwards Hill Road in Johnsburg were wonderfully and inextricably bound up with the Schaefer clan. Even these many decades hence, memories of those years play, as Francis "Cub" Schaefer would tell me in July 2000, like videotapes.

Many such scenes come from summers in Bakers Mills in the 1950s with The Rainmakers, our afore-mentioned band of avid young trout anglers. We named ourselves The Rainmakers part way through the summer, realizing that every time we *all* went fishing together, it rained.

The story opens with the whole troupe of us strung out along the diminutive stream through Johnny Robbins old place across Route 8, then from Johnny Steve's farm just south of the access lane off Route 8 into the Oehser camp east of Bakers Mills. We are all looking for likely fishing holes, meaning pools deep enough to keep a trout's dorsal fin from drying out. Willows overarch parts of the stream. All is idyllic until senior Rainmaker my brother Matt Zahniser comes crashing down the middle of the stream below some willows shouting "Bull! Run!"

He was not talking Civil War reenactment.

We all took off running in the direction Matt was headed, most of us having by then spotted the large bovine with horns who was running our direction. Cub took off sprinting for some distance but soon jettisoned his fishing rod—and somehow his glasses, too—then climbed a small tree to safety.

I was actually closest to Matt when the angry bovine first breathed down his neck and inspired him to cut and run shouting "Bull!" My immediate problem was that our mother Alice had insisted that morning that I must wear my "galoshes," or it was no fishing with the big kids for you, young man. Galoshes were rubber, over-shoe boots that fastened up to calf-level with metal clips. They were designed to slow down sprinters and keep safety-patrol kids dry at road intersections close to schools during suburban monsoons.

By the time I got to plodding along the stream toward the others, the bovine was so close behind me I could hear its breathing. The rest of The Rainmakers started shouting, "Cross the creek, Eddie. Cross the Creek!" In desperation, I made a 90-degree turn into three-inch-deep riffles and scooted onto the opposite bank. Miraculously, the bovine veered off. I no doubt owe my subsequent education, marriage, two children, and career to its aversion to getting the bottom-most portion of its hooves wet.

Matt later said he was *udderly* certain it was a cow, but it had horns and he thought the expletive "Bull!" would best get us Rainmakers in rapid motion out of harm's way.

The part of the story Cub edited out in later years was how he made Matt, who was 15-years-old to Cub's ten, go back into the Bull patch and fetch Cub's fishing rod and glasses. Cub's actual namesake was St. Francis, but, hey, tell that to Johnny Robbin's cow.

After Cub moved out West in the summer of 1962, I saw him again only in 1982 and again in 2000 in Jackson Hole. Both times the first topic of conversation had to be the "Bull!" Having re-run that story, we could then talk about our subsequent life events.

Soon after the summer of The Rainmakers, my brother Matt moved on to other things, like college and marriage, and I had more of Cub's attention to myself. Even before Matt graduated from The Rainmakers, however, Cub was generally our outdoors gear expert.

We four Zahniser kids grew up on hand-me-down L.L. Bean boots that we called "Packs." They have rubber bottoms and leather uppers. In those days you could send them back to Freeport, Maine and have new rubber bottoms quintuple-sewed to the enduring leather uppers in what, at our ages then, appeared to be perpetuity. That made them superb hand-me-downs for our family of four kids living on my father Howard Zahniser's paychecks from a relatively obscure nonprofit conservation group. For the duration of four kids, my parents never had to dispose of our Bean boots. They just bought a new pair for Matt, the oldest kid.

It didn't take long for Cub to scorn Bean boots in favor of some all-leather jobbies. And a couple years later, the only footgear one would be caught dead in the woods wearing were Peter Limmer boots. Cub assured us they were guaranteed for 2,000 miles even on rocky terrain. The thing was, by then Cub had quit growing, and my friend Larry Strausbaugh and I were still growing.

It was about time, people remarked, that Cub had grown into his feet. When Cub was 10 and 11 years old, had there been surfing in the Adirondacks, he could've done it without the board on the spacious soles of his tennis shoes.

The Herter's Inc. catalogs out of Waseca, Wisconsin carried a Bowie knife that looked a lot like an ordinary kitchen knife but could also be used, according to the always-ebullient Herter's catalog item descriptions, to cut eight-penny nails in half with the help of a hammer to drive the blade, which, by the way, would not then bend or nick.

Larry Strausbaugh and I quickly bought Herter's Bowie knives, but when we asked Paul Schaefer to test their sharpness at our cabin one night, Paul ran a finger over their edges and said they were both "dull as a hoe."

Larry and I were so crushed by Paul's curt judgment that Larry eventually specialized in new infectious diseases of internal medicine, and I majored in English.

Before Matt flew the nest, the Schaefer and Zahniser matriarchies and kids did a trek into the High Peaks so that the Schaefer women, particularly, could bag more 4,000-plus-foot peaks on their ways to becoming 46ers.

We trekked into the Flowed Lands area of the High Peaks with backpacks on this expedition that would spark the controversy, no doubt still raging somewhere, over who had the right to name the mountain that the female contingent of our expedition dubbed Shepherd's Tooth.

Schaefer means "shepherd," and Zahniser contains the root for "tooth."

Cub much preferred creeling trout to bagging peaks. Flowed Lands, the former human-made lake in the High Peaks served as our base camp. Cub had the brilliant idea that we could haul enough night crawlers and their sustaining dirt into our camp for ten days' worth of productive fishing. We hauled them in a bailed roofing-tar bucket, which pairs of us took turns carrying on a pole between our shoulders.

Lugging that awkward, heavy bucket of worms via pole on our shoulders, and stumbling along uneven trails, brought to our collective consciousness old television segments of "Rama of the Jungle."

The rub was that there turned out to be leeches in the Flowed Lands. Every time we plopped a fat, juicy, long-distance-trail-hauled nightcrawler anywhere near a High Peaks trout, the trout took off swimming like a hell-bent torpedo.

Cub remained my hero on that trip because he always carried a knife. I didn't. I wore a heavy black sweater every morning when we set out for more mostly fruitless fishing. By now, we used artificial flies, not worms. Flies tend to blow in the wind, and their barbs were great at my heavy black sweater. I was dependent on Cub—for that entire High Peaks trip—to cut my fishing flies out of my black sweater so I could return to fishing.

We caught the most trout on that trip in mostly small cascade pools of the outlet of Flowed Lands. I can still see those lively, back-watering pools now. I have repressed Cub's impatience with how my sweater cut into his own trout fishing time.

A later summer by brother Matt had the great luck to go to the Adirondacks in late spring with Paul and Grace Oehser. Ever after that he would tell me how much better the trout fishing was in the spring than in July and August, the post-black fly months our family usually logged at our cabin out of Bakers Mills. After Matt matured, he said he realized that the early summer with the Oehsers was the only time he'd done much fishing in the Adirondacks without Cub rushing ahead to hit all the best-looking pools first.

Larry Strausbaugh spent the summer in the Adirondacks with my mother, father, and me about 1959. He was totally enamored of Cub's effortless woodsmanship. For Cub, going fishing to Bog Meadow, Bog Meadow Falls on Round Pond Brook, and on down to Second Pond Flow was as nonchalant as for Larry and me to walk four blocks to the drugstore from our homes in the

Washington, D.C. suburbs then.

One day, Cub agreed to go fishing with Larry and me to those very locations. But first, he said, his Aunt Gertrude Fogarty had said he could go to the Fogarty cabin and make himself a peanut butter and jelly sandwich. With full gear in tow, Larry and I met Cub at the Fogarty's camp to go fishing. Well, not quite.

The Fogartys weren't there. We had to wait while Cub cleaned out entire jars of peanut butter and jelly and used more than half a loaf of bread making that proffered sandwich. For Larry and me, the suspense was arduous and continuous, because the sandwich Cub was eating, he would tell us, was the last one. But when he finished it he made the next one, regaling us with stories all the while.

We finally made it into the woods about mid-afternoon. There Cub taught us how to improve Adirondack trout waters by getting rid of chubs, feral bait-fish that were the bane of trout anglers. We ended up calling our removal process "derricking chubs." You could often tell by the feel of the strike that it was a chub and not a trout. If so, you lifted your fly rod and then gave it a sweeping pull back so that the chub exited the beaver pond and went flying past your head and shoulders just above the beaver-meadow grasses until you jerked your fly rod forward, snapping the chub off. Then it would flop in the beaver meadow grass and thereby improve trout fishing.

So went our so-called reasoning, at least.

This was great if you were as experienced and coordinated as Cub was. Larry and I were not always so. On the upstroke with our flyrods we sometimes flicked when we should've jerked, so that the chub came streaming back and slapped us in our faces. Even Cub could misfire sometimes, although with different consequence. One strike signaled "chub" to Cub and he went into derrick mode, only to see a larger fish roll over orange in the water. He knew he'd blown it on a nice brook trout. Cub didn't swear, but he could create a like aura with different words.

The greatest patience I ever remember Cub showing, besides cutting fishing flies out of my black sweater, was one night when he was on Edwards Hill alone and my mother invited him up to dinner. It was a Friday, and the Vatican still remembered its fish contract with the Hanseatic League then. My mother had forgotten about it being Friday and Cub being Catholic. She made a huge pot of Spanish rice with hamburger crumbled up in it. Cub sat there for two hours picking bits of ground beef out of his Spanish rice. Except for the modest mound of burger bits, he eventually cleaned his plate.

My mother felt terrible about this, but Cub kept picking away and saying "No problem."

The biggest food debate I ever had with Cub was actually with both he and his high school buddy Les on a trip we made to the High Peaks one August weekend in 1961. We ended up at Livingston Pond to fish its then nearly pristine waters. It soon dawned on me that I had been brought along to cook.

I was 15 and just back from six weeks in the Sheenjek River country of Alaska with Olaus and Mardy Murie, below the souther slope of Brooks Range. Later, we drove down to what is now Denali National Park, where we stayed with Adolph and Louise Murie.

On the High Peaks trip with Cub and Les, I had brought my square, cast-aluminum griddle. This was a good thing, because the only utensils we had were our small hunting knives. We cut woodchips with our ax to serve as a mixing spoon, and I had to flip our pancakes.

The big food debate, however, came over whether we should eat the humpbacked trout Cub caught in Livingston Pond. Cub, who by far outstripped Les and me for a compounding imagination, was convinced the trout hump was a tumor that could give us cancer. Les thought it might be a broken back that had healed crooked. But Cub's theory definitely spooked Les. I didn't know what to think, nor can I remember whether we ate that humpbacked trout.

The summers of my junior and senior years of high school I worked for Cub's father Paul and the Iroquois Hills construction outfit, living at the Schaefer homestead in Schenectady. The matriarch, Carolyn "Ma" Schaefer, was off those two summers cooking for the weather station on Whiteface Mountain. Evelyn, Monica, and I therefore took on all cooking duties for ourselves, Paul, and Cub.

Neither Ev, Monica, nor I were very experienced cooks, so we worked as a committee. Evelyn had some basic knowledge, Monica was good with a cookbook, and I had hung around my mother's cooking so doggedly that I knew what things were supposed to look like when "done." No matter that the Schaefer oven had only two settings—either *hot as hell* or *off*.

Every morning I made a huge batch of sourdough pancakes before Paul and I set off to work. Cub worked for Paul's mason Louie, so he set off by himself. Late in the summer I got up my nerve to try to bake a cherry pie. It was a big success, and Paul, Evelyn, Monica, and I each had small pieces.

Cub was out with his girlfriend and didn't get back until I had gone to bed in the loft of the Adirondack Room, which Cub and I shared. When I got up in the morning the pie pan was empty. When Cub got up, he said it had been a very good pie, even after he found out that I made it. I didn't bother to make another that summer.

One morning when Cub got up he asked me how I liked working with Paul's crew. I said fine. Cub said, "Well, are you sure? You were talking in your sleep last night complaining like crazy on and on about what a bad time the carpenters were giving you!" I swore him to silence.

Truth to tell, the crew could make you miserable, except for Uncle Nat

Keseburg and Louie the mason. They were good as gold and tried to take care of me all summer. The carpenters were eligible for "Good Citizenship" awards compared to the plasterers. Cub used to laugh when he was mixing mortar for Louie, and I was carrying the plaster that Uncle Nat was mixing for the plasterers, who were working in another room.

If Uncle Nat got the consistency of the plaster wrong, I caught holy hell from the plasterers, who had strings of foul invectives I had never imagined. They would also accuse me of going out with girls all night and doing all manner of lewd-sounding things, some of which I still have never heard of elsewhere—nor hope to.

Cub was full of brotherly advice for me on the job site, but I can't remember much of anything but the plasterers. No wonder builders use mostly drywall now.

One Saturday, Cub wanted to go climbing down in the Shawangunks and offered to take Monica and me along for the ride. Monica and I packed a large grocery bag full of food for lunch and dinner. The trouble was, we left that cornucopia of a grocery bag on the kitchen table. When we got to the 'Gunks, we realized our error. We each pulled out our money, and decided we had better divvy it up evenly. We each got 75 cents for food for the day.

Cub and Monica looked askance on my purchases. I bought two bananas and a large box of Milk Bone dog biscuits. I didn't go hungry. At one point, Monica—who carried her guitar everywhere she went then—was trying to get me to go sing with her for food in the campground. But Milk Bone trumps performance anxiety, and one box of those biscuits lasts a body a long time.

You may wonder why someone of Cub's size and speed never played high school football. Well, he explained to me that he had a condition the doctor just translated into plain English for him as "a soft head." If he took any sort of knock on the head, he said, it gave him excruciating headaches that lasted for days. So no football.

He was Paul Schaefer's son, so I didn't know whether to believe him, but it was true that Cub didn't play football. Of course, he didn't really need to. Long before high school, we had the complete "Bull!" story under our collective belts. What gridiron glories could match such an adventure? When I get to heaven, the first thing I'm going to do is put on my black sweater and go fly fishing, I'm sure Cub will be there with his knife to cut out my snags. But you can bet I'm not gonna fish anywhere near Johnny Robbins green pastures. No way. I plan to arrive on Friday. That night, Cub and I can go eat Spanish rice, and this time no pickin' out the burger bits. For dessert we can have peach ice cream and Milk Bone dog biscuits. Honest Cub, I'm just kidding.

"No problem."

High Peaks in Blowdown

As we made forays out from Mateskared, Schaefers were most often the way-showers and Zahnisers their eager followers. On their 1946 backpacking trip to Flowed Lands and Hanging Spear Falls on the Opalescent River in the High Peaks with Ed Richard, Paul Schaefer went so far as to carry my father Howard Zahniser on his shoulders across one difficult and hazardous approach by narrow ledge to the falls themselves. They then continued up through the boulder-strewn canyon of the Opalescent. Paul's accounts of the trip never mentioned that fact, gleaned from my father's journal. But it set a suitable tone for our families' joint wildlands outings.

My mother and we four kids would go off backpacking for trips of several days to a week with Carolyn and the Schaefer kids. Meanwhile, especially in the early years, Paul and Zahnie might be barnstorming for wilderness preservation around the Adirondacks. In the late 1940s, they rallied opposition to the series of dam projects that threatened Adirondack wilderness on Forest Preserve lands in the western Adirondacks.

On one trip back into the wilds adjoining Mateskared, our joint Zahniser and Schaefer clans plus Grace Oehser, without adult males, set up backpacking camp at Mud Pond, in what is now the New York State-designated Siamese Ponds Wilderness. The trip became multi-family famous for two of Grannie Grace's antics there. During the night, she had to get out of her sleeping bag at Nature's so-called prompting. Amidst this confined struggle—Grace was six feet tall—my mother Alice, sharing their pup tent, overheard an exasperated Grace muttering: *"Why doesn't someone invent a drop-seat sleeping bag?!"*

Grace was both artisan and artist, in skills and temperament. Her exasperations often expressed themselves in innovatively practical ways. In retrospect I'm surprised she didn't mock-up her drop-seat sleeping bag idea and sell it to L.L. Bean of Freeport, Maine.

Mud Pond is well back of beyond. One night, Alice and Grace convinced themselves, after the passle of us kids and Carolyn "Ma" Schaefer had dropped off to sleep, that they heard mature male voices nearby. To warn off any possible shenanigans hazardous to our women-and-children party, Grace and my mother took up a loud and supposedly spousal conversation. Grace played the exaggeratedly *basso profundo* husband whom my mother, in her usual speaking voice, but louder, addressed as "George".

Whether anyone else was nearby, we never knew, but their ploy, while we kids and Carolyn Schaefer slept, obviously worked, because no one bothered us.

On another night, Grace and my mother heard a bear munching down on blueberries right in the patch by which my sister Esther, unaware, lay in her sleeping bag.

In 1953, Carolyn convinced the four Schaefer kids that she and they should become "46-ers." This status could be claimed only by climbing all 46 Adirondack peaks over four thousand feet elevation. The 46-er tradition began with the indomitable Bob Marshall, his brother George, and their guide Herb Clark. One summer, they decided to do all these peaks and did. Subsequent measures of altitude have corrected the count of peaks that actually make it to four thousand feet or more, but the 46-er moniker has stuck.

Monica is the youngest Schaefer and younger than I am by several months. She was to become the youngest ever 46-er of her day and to hold the title for many years. Today that title has been pared down to first graders, maybe to pre-schoolers now, who probably play Suzuki violins and argue about Montessori educational methods as they climb.

Once having become 46-ers, the Schaefer women—Cub was usually engrossed in fishing—began to devise their own record schemes for the High Peaks. For example: Who could make the most ascents of Mt. Marcy barefoot? Mary Schaefer may still hold that record. The first-ever *recorded* ascent belongs to Ebenezer Emmons in 1837.

The summer of 1954, our Zahniser and Schaefer matriarchal contingents combined forces for a female peak-bagging expedition. The trip is recounted in Carolyn's book *The Schaefer Expeditions: 1953–1956*, privately printed by her family in 1989, with end-papers a hand-drawn map of "The High Peaks of the Adirondacks" by the late architect Frederic A. West. We base-camped at two Calamity Brook lean-to shelters within hollering distance of each other in the Flowed Lands area of the High Peaks. On this trip, an all-female Schaefer-Zahniser party climbed an apparently unnamed peak.

"Some of us hoped to climb 'Herbert-Clinton-Marshall.'" Carolyn later wrote of the trip, "we didn't know what to call it, but here we were and there it was. The only directions we could get were to climb by way of a stream that emptied into Flowed Lands. But, what stream?"

Setting off from the lean-tos they found a stream, but it proved to be the wrong one.

"For about a hundred feet it was nice going, and then we encountered blowdown. Being sure it was only temporary, we kept going over and under and along tree trunks for hours. We could hardly see the ground. The trees were like jackstraws, and we picked our way from tree to tree. But, underneath us we could see the friends' Irish setter wondering what we were doing up there. It was fascinating, but hopeless for a route up a mountain."

That was my brother Matt's dog, Rocky. Carolyn was not about to give up on a mountain. The next day the women decided to climb Iroquois and look over the situation. Carolyn writes:

"As we stood on top after signing our names in the register, we looked over at Herbert. 'It's a long way over there, but what's that little peak in between?' 'It's early in the day; let's see if we can get to that.' We went down to the end of Iroquois, tangling our hair in the spruce branches, getting down on our hands and knees to crawl beneath them, dropped down to the col, and found a corner to ascend the little peak, the only place we could see that was possible."

When I showed my wife Christine a few pictures from that trip, she remarked that "Women still wore head scarves then." Several wore bandanas tied over their hair—Carolyn on one summit with Monica, and at least Evelyn and probably my sister Esther at a rest stop in the thick of the blowdown. Christine hadn't had the benefit of reading Carolyn's account of tangled hair.

The intrepid climbers were on the unnamed mountain as Carolyn continues: "The top was like a little meadow and we sat down to eat our crackers and cheese. 'Where are the tin cans and bottles and candy wrappers? There aren't any around. Wonder how many people ever come over here.' We took out the map." There was no name for the peak.

I still recall how exhausted the climbing party looked when they got back to camp. On their no-trails approach and climb they fought blowdown from the 1950 storm that had leveled trees across 400,000 acres of the Adirondacks, leaving the woods full of downed trees stacked criss-crossed like the Devil's own obstacle course. Even Irish setter, Rocky, who could slink beneath much of the blowdown, came back utterly pooped. The boys—Cub Schaefer and my brother Matt and I—had opted to go fishing. Later, we could make no matching claims of piscatorial glory to distinguish our day.

How I forgot the incident of the day before I don't know, but Carolyn recounts it. Cub and Matt had set off to fish Calamity Pond, where Cub had caught two fine trout the year before.

"The two boys went down the trail with poles and tackle but soon were back," Carolyn wrote, "their eyes as big as saucers. 'What happened?' we asked. 'We saw two mountain lions crossing the stream! They had long tails!'"

As Carolyn calmly reports: "The next day they went fishing again."

Fishing was mostly a disaster from the start for that entire High Peaks trip. Determined to supplement camp fare with plenteous trout, we brought in such gobs of nightcrawlers we had to carry them in a large, bail-handled utility bucket. Worms, dirt, and bucket weighed so much we ended up carrying the bucket suspended from a pole set between two people's shoulders. This is not a convenient posture on rock-strewn trails when you are also burdened with your backpack.

To add insult to injury, the first time we cast bait from our hard-won worm cargo toward those High Peaks trout, they scattered in fright. They would no more take our luscious nightcrawlers than wait belly-up on the water's surface to sacrifice themselves to a great blue heron. As near as we could figure out, our night crawlers looked too much like leeches for the trout's comfort. After a couple days of scaring trout, we admitted defeat and abandoned the worms. The few trout the three of us caught that trip were fooled by artificial flies Matt had brought. Perhaps trout are simply conservative feeders, and the High Peaks probably hadn't seen a native nightcrawler since before the last Ice Age.

Because we could not glut ourselves on fresh trout, the Zahniser lean-to ran out of every edible but our staple starch, white rice, before the end of the trip. We were far too proud to let on to the Schaefer lean-to that we had provisioned poorly. So, for two days or so we ate nothing but rice. My mother cooked it in whatever ways she could imagine to keep this mono-diet palatable. We ate rice with reconstituted powdered milk and brown sugar for breakfast, balls of rice for lunch, and rice patties for dinner. Matt was the senior male in our two camps, and his fishing assumed a determined character but still returned next to nothing.

Rice it was, and the closest I ever came to a macrobiotic diet, which I had not heard of then—and only if white rice should qualify as macrobiotic.

Canon Cook, The Mother

Our mother Alice should be canonized for all the meals she cooked over open wood fires—a patron saint of Outdoor Cookery. I was in the Army in Korea during the summer that Mateskared finally plugged into the electric power grid, to take up at last the promise of that pole standing patiently next to our outhouse for our then 22 years of ownership with only apparent utility. Previously, those two decades plus of cooked meals served at Mateskared were cooked over open wood fires, whether indoors or outdoors. So too were all cooked meals served while our family backpacked on forays into what is now the Siamese Ponds Wilderness or in the High Peaks region, not to mention wilderness travels out West. Like a proverbial army, we backpackers march on our stomachs. Just so were untold family adventures made not only possible but successful mostly through my mother's willing spirit for outdoor cookery.

Cooking over open wood fires is a complex task. As with martial arts, certain discipline and knowledge are requisite. You must move beyond them in actual practice, however, to succeed. You must react according to the demands and pace set by the environment, including the properties of the wood fire and its fuel.

You must know the cooking properties not only of your various foodstuffs but of the wood fuel, whether hardwood or softwood, dry or somewhat wet. You must be patient. You must wait for the proper stage in the fire's life cycle and then exploit it full-tilt. You must exploit the fire's center and edges to coordinate the varied heats demanded by an entree and side dishes. Inevitably, you must also nurture and coax the fire along with the most fitting sticks of wood at hand, neither losing the fire nor raising a scorching blaze that frustrates all your patience to that point.

All this my mother knew. I can still have visual memories of her routine indoors and out at Mateskared. Her long-handled wooden spoon might shoot out to nudge a kettle or skillet an inch or two or three left or right to avoid or exploit a flare-up brought on by a shift of the breeze.

When Jerome Kern and Otto Harbach wrote their song "Smoke Gets in Your Eyes" for their 1933 musical *Roberta*, my mother was still in high school. The duo may have confused love with cooking over an open fire. So did my mother. Her willingness for wilderness cookery opened up whole new worlds of magical outdoor experience for us kids.

Paul Schaefer's Headwaters Faith

As a builder of Adirondack cabins, conservationist Paul Schaefer did not consistently solve the problem of water supplies. Around 1950, Paul had a well dug in front of his old log cabin on the the Cragorehol property downhill from our family cabin, Mateskared. Paul told me he bought the 100-year-old cabin—then sited elsewhere—and moved it here before I was born. The well still provides delicious, cold water, although the cabin no longer exists. The main, extended Fogarty family cabin — formerly owned by Paul's and his siblings' parents — now has its water pumped in by electric pump from its own, drilled well. Many years ago, we kids helped carry the well water in buckets over to Cragorehol camp—quite the laden tromp for youngsters.

I walked Liz Thorndike and her former Cornell University student Kristin Ruether over to Paul's old log cabin one September day. They wanted to see where the young Paul Schaefer dreamed his early wilderness preservation dreams. Too often we think of our conservation forebears as older men and women with white hair, but they all experienced starting-out. When Paul Schaefer met Bob Marshall atop Mount Marcy in the early1930s, Paul would then have been little more than Kristin Ruether's age the day we visited the cabin site. Paul was on Marcy with his camera to document a pressing conservation problem. It was what he knew to do then. Paul's conservation mentor John Apperson taught Paul to stand at any place he wanted to save and to photograph it so people could see what's at stake.

Liz Thorndike was then a visiting fellow at Cornell University, teaching a wilderness course in its traditionally utilitarian Department of Natural Resources. Kristin had taken Liz's course the year before. Liz also served as a trustee of the Association for the Protection of the Adirondacks—now Adirondack Wild: Friends of the Forest Preserve—the organization Paul Schaefer served as vice president for forty years.

I looked at the fieldstone chimney on Paul's old log cabin. Possibly George Morehouse built it. It was so like our George Morehouse-built chimney at Mateskared, although smaller on Paul's old one-story log cabin.

"I thought wells were always round," Kristin remarked. Ah youth, with its penchant to front the obvious.

I looked down into the well, given Kristin's question. Indeed, it is like a greatly enlarged fieldstone chimney rising from below ground. My memory of the well—going back to 1950—would have pegged it as round. I should have majored in biology like Kristin, to sharpen my perception. Kristin would go on to receive her J.D. from Lewis and Clark Law School and to serve as senior staff attorney with the Western Watersheds Project. Her legal work has kept livestock grazing out of Washington State wildlife areas and influenced grazing decisions in Wilderness Study Areas.

Part of Paul's problem with cabin water sources may have been that he didn't relish fooling with electric pumps. Scooting up to Bakers Mills from Schenectady, you don't want to spend your time fooling with pumps and other such impediments to the laid-back contemplative life. Paul made those scoots north to Bakers Mills, Cragorehol, and his old log cabin for decades before the Adirondack Northway segment of Interstate highway was built in the 1960s.

Paul also had great faith in gravity, a sort of headwaters faith. Maybe it was mixed in with his enormous regard for Verplanck Colvin's having identified the Hudson River headwaters on Mount Marcy in what Colvin named "Lake Tear of the Clouds." The upshot was that Paul spent considerable time looking for the perfect spring uphill of his most recent cabin projects. I don't know how many hundreds of feet of black plastic piping I got involved in running across the landscape from likely springs down to the Beaver House cabin Paul built in the 1960s below Mateskared. We ran more down to his cabin he built on the Chatiemac Road in the mid-1960s.

How Paul so readily located specific things in the woods was a mystery to me until, post-Army, Christine and I came to Mateskared in spring, before trees leafed out. It was a revelation, how far we could see into the woods. Paul tramped all through here in late fall's hunting season, after the leaves were off deciduous trees.

One day in the early 1960s, Paul gathered us to help dig out a spring he'd found down and across our road between Mateskared and the Beaver House. Where our road begins its steepest descent halfway between our cabin and the end of the hardtop at Camp Triumph, Paul led us about fifty feet west into the woods. Paul's brother-in-law, Ed Fogarty and Ed's son David took part. The spring Paul had located emerged below a rock nearly the size of a contemporary Volkswagen Beetle then. We cut out a pooling basin with a hatchet and shovels and were not greatly impressed with how slowly the water pooled up. But we ran the piping down to the Beaver House through the second-growth woods.

Paul would dicker with other potential Beaver House waterworks that wouldn't pan out. In Paul's last years, he settled for piping in water from the stream that flows under Edwards Hill Road from the former Dalaba Hillmount Farms onto his property. He picked up the head of flow below our barn at Mateskared. But it's now problematic to drink untreated surface water, so the Beaver House solution wasn't really a potable solution.

My brother Matt and I once traced the present piping uphill from the road. In some places, turf and root masses had claimed it in the power line right of way. The power company keeps that stretch clear of tall trees and creates a tangle of shrubs and stump-sprouting trees. Matt and I scouted dead ahead whenever we lost the piping. We found its headwaters surprisingly close to Mateskared's barn—as though Verplanck Colvin had searched for the Hudson River source only to find it near his home in Albany.

Pieces of board raised the water level of a small, shallow pool and walled three sides. The board cover and rock meant to submerge the pipe were dislodged. We re-jigged things and cleaned the improvised filter screen. We scooped out cold pool-bottom sediment, the better to bury the pipe head.

We recoupled all pipe-clamp joints we could find, but back at the road culvert still found no flow. We had to ask Leland Morehouse to come make it work. But Matt and I now knew why the Beaver House piping flows with a healthy head of pressure. How might Verplanck Colvin have felt, had he traveled to see the Hudson River's outflow at New York City.

Over many years, I would grasp how deeply Colvin's example influenced Paul Schaefer. It might explain Paul's delight when he, his nephew Michael Fogarty, and I "discovered" that the State of New York owned Nate Davis Pond. The pond did not appear on topographic quadrangles or state maps, although it lies just south of Bakers Mills. The state didn't know it existed or that the state owned it.

Paul's enthusiasm for our small-scale exploration of discovery points to why we need to keep wilderness and wildness alive in the world. Paul's delight paralleled Bob Marshall's 1930s sense of discovery high on Mount Doonerak in Alaska's mountain kingdom that Marshall named Gates of the Arctic. Both no doubt resonated to Colvin's sense of discovery at Lake Tear in the 1870s. In 1966, Paul would write of Nate Davis Pond in *The Living Wilderness* magazine:

The lake is situated in the bowl of several small mountains, off the beaten path, and is reached by climbing up through a mixed forest where huge canoe birches predominate. The outlet of the lake goes over a rock ledge and its stream goes into a heavy swamp before entering the open hardwoods and dropping to the valley where it crosses a dead-end road into a large tract of the Forest Preserve. The lake, at about 2000 feet elevation, probably about 25 feet deep, has been known to a few mountaineers only. By a strange coincidence, descendants of the original settlers in the area, living less than three miles airline down the valley, never heard of it.

When Paul's article appeared, the state conservation department had verified that it indeed "owned" the lake. Perhaps Paul Schaefer's headwaters faith was simply that any stream implies its headwaters.

Let Sleeping Cabins Lie

If someone would poke out the eyes of the hawks
We sparrows could dance wherever we please
   —-Cold Mountain

In the soul's delicious fog between our sleep and full wakefulness, consciousness emerges like a sly ventriloquist. Moving freely about the stage, it takes full advantage of the blurry atmospherics. These August mornings on the cabin porch, when my sons emerge from their cabin sleep, I try to blend my voice with this ventriloquism. It's a parent's only hope of revising the coding errors of our contributions to their DNA.

How often we know far better than we manage to do. If wisdom were a basketball hoop it would be 15 feet off the ground, not the standard 10 feet. I probe my sons' inner fogs: "Wisdom is knowledge lived over time," I say.

Nothing. Like a weak headlight beam I have just discounted my own wisdom penetrating our early morning consciousness. Poor timing.

The boys sit transfixed, staring at the mountain. One nice thing about this interlude of awareness is how the act of disrespect otherwise implied by ignoring a parent's direct address is necessarily suspended. I imagine we may not see this particular suspension of the dogma of respect again until they visit me in the nursing home some day.

You will visit me, won't you?

Fog, mist, and cloudiness attend our borders and transitions. Out near Crane Mountain morning mists nestle like lakes in low-lying valleys. When ancient Greeks boarded Charon's ferry to cross the River Lethe's waters of forgetfulness to the shore of death, don't you imagine something other than a sunny, blue-sky day?

Maybe post-night sleep's inner fog is what some call the Alpha state. My sons do seem caught up in meditative bliss. So much for spiritual effort. Early on, even the Bible gives only simplest instruction: "See, I have put before you today life and death. Choose life."

How arduous is that—as instruction, I mean?

Or: "Sleepers awake!" How's that for a two-word manual for the religious life? It's as easy as One, Two, Alpha State. Two words hardly less fraught with complex meaning. Or Psalm 46: "Be still and know that I am God."

If God played straight with Moses on the mountain before Godself sent Moses back to Egypt, that verse might better be punctuated: "Be still and know that I Am, God."

What I like about this time of day is how you can get away with asking your kids the really tough, deep questions of life: "If there's an Alpha state, what is the Omega state?"

Nothing. The guys are still tight-rope walking on their own fixed gazes somewhere between the cabin porch and Crane Mountain. Mind over Matter is kid's stuff compared to No-mind over Matter. The quality of the fog is such that you can't tell whether the one emerging is an adult or a young person.

(Later today, out of the supposed blue, Justin answers that "Alpha state-Omega state" question with: "The nursing home." Blank minds record best.)

In the Galapagos Islands, night-feeding white gulls often follow boats. Boats produce food scraps, and they churn up seawater, bringing natural food close to the surface. These land-based birds emerge from near darkness like flitting ghosts. Local lore prizes the gulls as good luck charms. At early morning, they fly back to land, and a lost boat could follow them. Open ocean horizons are featureless, like inner fog or the mind at utter rest.

Abjectly different circumstances can work the clear mind like fog does. Witness Darwin in the Galapagos Islands recasting life's slow unfolding. Three years on a boat away from home and you go crazy. That, or you focus, focus, focus. From a different island but what looks like the same bird, only with more curve to its beak—suddenly what everyone so long ignored about the good monk Gregor Mendel's genetic theory makes stone-cold sense to Darwin.

"The only one who cannot be awakened," I tell my sons, "is the one who only pretends to sleep."

They still struggle for balance on their own gazes out across to Crane Mountain. What you depart from is not the way. Balance, balance.

Today's cyberized wisdom is advertised as an easy nut to crack, Cosmic Egg as shell game, wisdom as knowledge over-easy. There's chicken soup for your soul and a mere half of the truth of Hinduism plunked into western consumer culture by a former baggage handler from India. Think positive: if something bad happens, it's your own fault. You weren't thinking positive.

But here's some chicken soup for your soul. Will that be for here or to go?

The soup or my soul?

A small cloud mass differentiates itself to the cabin's port side, just off the bow. It looks like a white gull, headed toward the mountain. Off their tightropes now, my sons watch the gull, too. Another day is auspiciously launched here on the edge of wilderness.

The Ice Meadows

I phoned Evelyn from the grocery store in North Creek to talk over the logistics of the day's projected expedition to what Evelyn calls "the Ice Meadows" located along the Hudson River downstream of the Glen highway bridge on Route 28. The upshot was that my sister Esther and her husband Duncan Gillies and my wife Christine and I agreed to meet Evelyn and her younger sister Monica there. Monica and husband Wayne Wiitanen were in the Adirondacks from Michigan, for a weekend Schaefer family reunion. Wayne was a former owner, with Evelyn's sister, Mary Schaefer, and Evelyn's then future husband Don Greene, of the old Putnam Farm at the base of Crane Mountain.

The Ice Meadows do not show as such on topographical maps. To the untrained eye—mine would be one—they look like rather ordinary, rocky river flats. But on closer examination, several anomalous phenomena set them apart.

First, there are no trees as you would normally think of trees. Second, such trees as exist are maintained at mere shrub proportions, possibly by the river ice that names the meadows. Deer might also crop them—Evelyn had been trying to puzzle out this and several other phenomena.

"I've seen evidence only once," she said. Looking via hand-lens at "some scraped ash sprouts" there once, however, she concluded it evidenced mouse chewings. When they might do this was still a mystery to her. "Not under the ice, and I have never seen any other sign of them out there. There's no place to hide, but it's true that mice explore a lot. But they should eat bark only in winter." Evelyn then recalls a specific winter: "It's true the frazil ice didn't clog until December 11."

Neither the white ash nor the alder, few though they are, grow to more than two and a half feet tall. And they grow as clumps of shoots not by unitary tree trunks. In the case of the white ash, the woody stems appear to have died off about two and a half feet from the ground. They don't really look as though ice had snapped them off or deer had chewed them off. The alder is far more supple than the ash—perhaps aping the Taoist idea that grass is more powerful than stone because it gives and therefore endures. Alder doesn't seem to die back at two and a half feet above the ground in the Ice Meadows, but neither does it seem to grow to more than that height.

Evelyn did locate possible signs of abrading, as though by ice action, on lower areas of the alder stems at the interior of a clump. But ground-level abrading can't be the issue at the Ice Meadows. As you stand at river level here, you look up at the forest edge 15 or more feet above the slope of the high riverbank and the flood plain and see what look like blazes on the trees. The blazes are big enough that, were they oven pans, you could bake a batch of brownies in them.

"That's not the work of Boy Scouts," Evelyn said of the bark scars. Evidently, the ice really backed up on the river here in 1956. What look like blazes mark the level at which the ice's freeze-hardened crust scraped the bark off trees at the forest's edge.

A car we could see parked on the road across the river from us would have been a candidate for being displaced as an automotive glacial erratic. Such a massive jumble of ice clearly would have overridden that road.

Not all of this is your ordinary river ice. The proper term is *frazil* ice. In her attempts to understand this ice and its role in specifying the very particular flora of the Ice Meadows, Evelyn, who was becoming visibly passionate about this bit of our planetary ecology, consulted both ice engineers and meteorologists.

It would make better drama to say these experts pooh-poohed each other's opinions, but Evelyn consulted the ice engineers first. It was the meteorologists, therefore, who pooh-poohed the ice engineers' theories.

"I took internationally known ecologist Daniel Botkin to an ash tree, and he was intrigued and puzzled, too," Evelyn said. "He wanted the tops to be sticking out above the ice all winter. I took a picture of one single stem sticking out above the frazil, and two minutes later after a mile of river had let loose piling frazil up, that stick was well covered. Was that an exciting day! I was standing two feet above and four feet from the spot that chunks of ice crashed into the ledge. I had moved a few feet up out of the way before it really got moving. This was the first day the frazil had backed up to near The Glen. Before it settles down, there's much shoving of huge areas against others."

Frazil ice forms from super-cooled water and may form first in the air above the river water, with a nucleation. Crystals need a nucleus around which then can crystallize. That nucleation somehow gets the ice ball rolling, really rolling. River neighbors here have gone to bed with the river clear of ice and awakened the next morning to find it frozen across with frazil ice already quite deep.

"One study I have finally gotten my hands on—on microfiche, and they sent a portable machine too!—tells about making frazil in the lab by spraying water over supercooled water," Evelyn said, "the droplets freezing and nucleating frazil, for Pete's sake!"

A common name for frazil ice is "bacon ice." It is white on top and gray farther down, like the cooled skim of rendered bacon fat: call this the Hudson Lardstream. The term *frazil* comes from the French-Canadian language, Beat novelist Jack Kerouac's native tongue. It means "cinders."

"It's supposed to look like cinders," Evelyn explained, "but bacon grease is a better comparison. It really looks like bacon grease."

I did not have the nerve to ask Evelyn whether she thought these folks might be pulling her leg when suggesting this peculiar ice phenomenon was hardening their arteries.

The freezing point of water is 32 degrees Fahrenheit. For frazil ice to form the air temperature needs to be 25 degrees. "The water only gets to -.01 to -.08 Celsius"—Evelyn kindly translated that for me to 31.86 Fahrenheit—which is the problem for the ice engineers. Ice shouldn't nucleate in water until the water is four or five degrees colder. Rapids help cool water by capturing cold air and by getting rid of the latent heat released by freezing—and rapids make bubbles, of course. (One plant expert Evelyn consulted has observed that ice meadows occur on rivers that have rapids.) The river motion prevents the water from crystallizing at 32 degrees. This over- readiness to freeze no doubt contributes to the ability of frazil ice to fill the river overnight.

"Twenty-five degrees, right you are, let's get on with it!"

Evelyn has stood and watched the stuff grow—which is what crystals actually do, they grow.

I have read of similar rapid freezing that takes place in forms of surface ice that seem to work almost like chain reactions once one ice crystal succeeds in forming. In such cases, winter freeze-up would be equally as dramatic as spring breakup. Henry Thoreau was greatly fascinated by the similarity of leaf structures and crystal structures. It was a fascination he picked up in part from German writer Johann Wolfgang von Goethe.

Perhaps it was an ice engineer who enlightened the plant geneticist *cum* plant engineer who many years ago now spliced an antifreeze gene from a coldwater fish into a tomato. The gene purports to make it possible to store the tomato at a low temperature without damaging its texture. The direct action of the gene is to prevent the formation of ice crystals, an important consideration for the living tissue of that antifreeze-gene host fish of far northern waters.

That's what the Hudson Lardstream needs to combat frazil ice, something to prevent the formation of crystals in winter. But it is precisely the formation of the crystals, how their nucleation first occurs, that challenged Evelyn and her consulting experts.

"Because of the super cooling of the water, things are going on in the rapids," Evelyn explained. "The surface of the water is capturing cold air and taking it into the water."

She was warming up to the bubble theory put forth by an expert on bubble physics.

"The bubble person spoke about thousands of micro droplets per bubble bursting in the air" above the rapids.

A meteorologist agreed the bubble person could be correct. Even the ice engineer did a sort of flip-flop then.

"Later in the winter the ice engineer, when I contacted him, called me back and said, 'Sure, that could be it. Ice bubbles.'"

No doubt you can make frazil ice in a lab. You can even clone a sheep now. But it may be that you can't know how frazil ice clogs the Hudson River just below the Glen unless you've been with this place over time, as Evelyn Greene has.

"I think Snake Rock is necessary in the first clogging of the river. Opposite the rock an eddy freezes and builds out into the river. Eddies are very important in clogging frazil. The great masses of frazil floating down the river, thickly and inexorably on a cold day, get squeezed into huge rafts, which are somewhat congealed. The rafts get wedged-in when they must get around this curve at the Ice Meadows. *Voila*, the next morning the river is six feet deep in ice. Though all of this can happen in the daytime if it is cold enough—and these eyes have seen it done."

Howard Zahniser with Eleventh Mountain in the background. Photo by Ed Zahniser

Hooper Mine

[Pix at https://blogs.agu.org/magmacumlaude/2012/07/16/hooper-garnet-mine/
Jessica Ball is a volcanologist at the USGS — blogs.agu.org]

Hooper Mine, a former garnet operation, lies near the Garnet Hill Lodge above Thirteenth Lake. Evelyn Schaefer Greene first introduced our family to Hooper Mine in the heyday of our son Justin's interest in rocks and minerals. Evelyn also bushwhacked with us to visit a tough-to-find, very old and small graphite mine near Johnsburg.

The regrowth hardwood forest on the hillside leading up to Hooper Mine shows evidence of relict machinery and other metal artifacts of a former fixed and industrious human presence. The mine itself greets you as an open, roughly rectangular pit with incised cliffs of varying heights on most of three sides. It forms an unnatural amphitheater. Chunks of garnet lie everywhere embedded in standing rock and the slag and scree at the bases of the human-cut cliffs.

Decades on, now Justin still likes to visit Hooper Mine every summer and whack the rocks with our masonry hammer. So do I. It renews my optimistic side, which is not reflexively optimistic in the sense that, for example, I am right-handed.

Crystals of garnet look deceptively as though they might pop right out of their rock substrate at you. As Buddhists might say: "First thought, best thought." But no such luck. The dull, metallic *thunk* of the masonry hammer's bladed end assailing the rocks is lucky to chip off even a healthy garnet flake. No way do nuggets pop out of the rocks. I can't imagine what hard, hand labor went into early garnet mining. Nor can I quite imagine creating Hooper Mine's huge, flat-floored pit from its former profile as suggested by its current walls.

On one visit to Hooper Mine, we encountered a mountain search-and-rescue training session in progress. The team lowered a rescue litter lines anchored to the mine pit's opposing cliff tops. Even given an emergency, I would no more relish riding that jerking, sliding litter than I would agree to ride The Great Escape Amusement Park's "Steamin' Demon" roller coaster.

Hooper Mine's leveled floor oddly combines dry conditions and pooled rainwater that cannot drain from the bedrock. All manner of insects and garter snakes are about. No doubt the latter eat the former. A few tree saplings have taken hold, but sparsely. Walking across parts of the pit floor on jumbled slag is like walking stone-cobbled willow and alder flats along Wyoming's Snake River in Jackson Hole. No doubt the light projecting through sparse sapling stands and the vegetation's aroma trigger such comparison. Or perhaps the marsh-like plant with elongated seed heads that look like spiked caterpillars.

I associate those seed heads with beaver ponds in the flats near the Snake River there. In 1954, using his flyrod, my father and I enticed trout to rise for those seed heads after we lost the two hooks my father had brought. A later summer in the Adirondacks, with my fly-tying vise, I lashed similar seed heads to long-shanked streamer fishhooks. Fished like dry flies, those improvised lures caught trout. My father had once caught sunfish by the swim beach at Lake Minerva, using rounded white blossoms of a pearly everlasting flowers as bait. Go in quest of garnet gems at Hooper Mine, and there is no telling what your memory may snag.

To reach Hooper Mine, we drive beyond North Creek up along the Hudson River to the community of North River, as the river itself is known there. We then take Thirteenth Lake Road up a charming creek valley to the Garnet Hill Lodge ski barn. From there hike about a half-mile, moderate climb through re-growth hardwood forest up to the mine. Handmade wooden signs direct you toward the mine so you don't mistakenly take the lodge's nature trail down the hillside.

Hooper Mine's quarry pit is perhaps a football field's length at its greatest extent, from where the access trail debouches into it out to its far wall to your right. A few low rock ridges run out into it, the odd rock here and there, and its flat floor has a generally rocky, talus-like composition. Otherwise the quarry could be imagined as a small football stadium. The press box would be atop the downslope stand of cliff that rises perhaps 80 feet off the quarried-out playing field.

What would most challenge football teams would be the saplings taking hold on their playing surface. These are mostly a birch-and-poplar succession with here and there a white pine, cedar-like conifer, spruce, ash, or maple. The maples appear to be doing least well now, but given enough time, despite the poor drainage, they might well win the day and dominate the Hooper Mine forest canopy. In so doing they might not even rise above the pit's rim.

On this day it was wet underfoot after days of steady rain. A garter snake 10 to 12 inches long revealed itself before gliding under a rock like an ostrich sticking its head in sand. Long after its head disappeared, I could have picked up the snake, as most of remained in full view. Tiny toads also were out and about. No doubt the snake would rather be eating them than idling in supposed hiding from me.

The mine floor's watery substrate also pushed up moisture-loving sedges—with spiky-caterpillar looking seed heads—and the ancient plant species, *Equisetum*. We call it horsetail, or joint grass. Its stalk grows in bamboo-like sections that pop apart easily with a satisfying sound that mesmerized me as a kid. Its stalk feels synthetic, machined almost. Joint grass would have felt at home at Hooper Mine in Carboniferous times. No doubt somewhere its ancestors now generate electricity as hard coal.

I was not entirely surprised to find a carnivorous plant growing on the floor of the Hooper Mine pit. Meat-eating plants tend to show up where the soil nitrogen content is too low for most plants' nutritional needs. Carnivorous plants, such as sundew and pitcher plant, get their needed nitrogen from insects. At Hooper Mine, given its rock substrate, soil is sporadic and still thin. During drought the mine floor might be very dry as well, sedges, horsetails, and saplings notwithstanding. The sundew gets its name from the beads of liquid that adorn it. Insects mistake the sundew's beads for drops of water. They are instead a sticky fluid that first secures and then ingests the hapless insect.

Many years ago, Justin and Eric and I took my brother-in-law Duncan Gillies up to Hooper Mine. Duncan, my late sister Esther's husband, is a Scotsman and a gardener who has long lived in London. "You have to know how big some of these trees could get in another hundred years," I suggested to him on the trail up to the mine, "to realize we are walking through forest still recovering from relatively recent logging or clearing for agriculture or mining."

White birches prove the point. For many years, I assumed that making a birchbark canoe was a quilter's task—stitching together small sheets of bark. Not so. Most birches near our cabin are modest sized re-growth trees now still recovering formerly cleared land. The 24- and 32-foot-long fur-trade canoes used from Canada's St. Lawrence River west to Winnipeg and beyond were usually fabricated from the bark of one big birch tree. John McPhee describes this in *The Survival of the Bark Canoe*. Folds in the trunk's massive bark sheet might be stitched and pitched, but the overall process was not like quilting. Imagine portaging such weighty behemoths and their supplies and fur payload bundles over continental water divides.

I should declare my bias: I love the birch. It keeps its eyes on you in the woods. Watch for the birch eyes, rounded, dark, and topped by black, seemingly arching eyebrows. A hymn or chant for these trees might be called "Canticle for Lenticles," the latter being the term for birchbark's eye-like features.

Only clouds and shelf fungi bellies rival this birch's white bark in summer. Sun-struck stands makes mental pictures worth framing. Vincent Van Gogh would stop long and stare hard. Not that aesthetic delight blinds me to the birch's utility. Its resinous bark burns a smoky black like the diesel fuel we burned in Army space heaters in Korea during the "Viet Nam Conflict." Many rainy backwoods treks have been redeemed—meal-wise, comfort-wise, and gear-drying—by wet firewood urged ablaze by birchbark.

Tea connoisseurs, please know that the birch tree's springtime leaf buds can be steeped for an infusion like tea leaves. Picking the resin-rich leaf buds is a stickiness challenge but worth the effort. Be warned: if you use a tea infuser (aka "tea ball") with a screw-on lid, do not overfill it. The leaf buds will so swell by steeping they will jam the lid tight.

What Crane Mountain Said

I made a pond for the moon.
—Stonehouse

In geological lore, Crane Mountain is a monolith, "one rock." From our Mateskared cabin porch, Crane is "the view." Up close and personal, Crane harbors a pond. The summit once had a staffed fire tower, but aircraft surveillance and then satellite monitoring obsoleted that. As a monolith or "one rock," Crane reduces our nearby Big Rock to lesser proportions than our yard rocks—the Stone Throne of the Acting Rock—or like the mica flakes and garnet bits in old road gravels here.

Until I saw Half Dome and El Capitan in Yosemite National Park in California, I found it difficult to grasp Crane as one rock, partly because forests and blueberry plants cover so much of Crane. When I sit up there and look across the pond to low cliffs on the far shore, the scene suggests a normal beautiful environment. Can this so diverse scene be set on one rock? But, is not all Earth one rock—its bump-and-grind lithosphere, at least? We are all campers and sojourners on one rock?

Crane inspires such thoughts. Bill McKibben once lectured in the Adirondack Discovery series about Crane Mountain in literature. In his book *The Age of Missing Information,* he contrasts his experience watching *all* one weekend's TV programming available in the Washington, D.C. suburb of Fairfax, Virginia, with his experience spending a weekend on a mountain that he calls Crow. At Mateskared, in full view of Crane Mountain, I once read an early Paul Schaefer manuscript. It recounts Paul's solo winter backpacking expedition afoot from his old log cabin here off Edwards Hill Road out of Bakers Mills and across to climb up Crane, staying overnight. The pond seemed aptly frozen, so Paul started walking across it. But, he was soon inspired to move briskly along as pond ice started to crack with his every footstep. Paul's winter Crane trek now appears in his book *Adirondack Cabin Country*.

I often image Crane Mountain Pond as a mystic third eye set in the one-rock monolith and trained on the heavens—what many primal cultures knew as "the dome of sky." Celestial regards. Earth and heaven conjunct.

In the United States Southwest, rock pockets that hold rainwater into the dry season are called *tinajas.* They keep many species of wildlife alive through the thirsty times. Imagine Crane's pond as once a humongous rock pocket filled with glacial ice and whose water level is today maintained by precipitation that counters its evaporative and modest outlet losses. Given time enough—"Hello, heavens!"— the pond outlet should carve its way into the mountainside and drain the pond.

Do not hold your breath against that day.

You would not theorize such erosion from zero knowledge of geomorphology, Earth's penchant for shape-changing. Based solely on one August day's observations, you would not predict this pond-draining scenario unless you were 1800s Swiss scientist Louis Agassiz on a roll. Agassiz first championed the theory—developed in his homeland's Alps—that the glaciers of an Ice Age, and not a Biblical flood, had shaped much of Earth's northern latitudes.

Agassiz's early ardent American apostle glaciologist was John Muir. Muir first discovered actual living glaciers in California's Sierra Nevada—and did battle with formidable California State Geologist Josiah D. Whitney. Muir flew in the face of the then dominant gradualist geological orthodoxy: Glaciers shaped Yosemite Valley, Muir said, not the Biblical flood.

Whitney publicly called Muir "an ignorant sheepherder"—Muir had shepherded sheep for a time in Yosemite—culpable of deluding uneducated people. In fact, Muir was substantially correct, and Agassiz was vindicated for future American science.

When people wax dogmatic today about how this planet works, remember that Muir and Whitney duked it out *after* the Civil War, around the time my grandparents were born. (My grandparents would have sided not with Muir or Whitney but with Bishop Ussher's claim that God created the world in 4004 BCE, starting after dusk on Saturday, October 22.)

In August, Crane Mountain Pond's outlet often reads as mere glissade, a sliding gossamer sheet wide as your outspread hand from pinkie tip to thumb tip. Only limnologists or hydrologists would even think to gauge the glissade's depth—or perhaps Henry Thoreau re-incarnate. Crane Pond, that is, will not drain by gradualist erosion in your lifetime. Better to bet on earthquakes. Or better yet on a polar shift flip-flopping the Adirondacks and Australia to make the water fall out down under!

Crane Mountain lies just inside the next quadrangle south of our former Thirteenth Lake—now Bakers Mills—topographical map. After my father Howard Zahniser died in 1964, Paul Schaefer convinced my mother Alice and me that he should cut a picture window into Mateskared's south wall. My father's attitude toward the cabin was that paying real estate and school taxes sufficed for maintenance. And not improving anything reduced maintenance too. Nor would you hazard spending yearly vacations repairing defects that your earlier improvements set in motion.

Sociologically, the picture window was a plus. More people could sit in the front room and simultaneously stare at Crane. At one point the couch got placed with its back to the picture window, and up to four people were forced to seem more interested in life inside the cabin than in staring at Crane. No problem: My mother, three siblings, and wife all trained as counselors. The couch again sits along the interior wall, facing the fieldstone fireplace.

For many years pre-parenthood, I kept a meditation regimen that would dovetail with my interest in mountain writings. One summer, with parenthood launched, I did an extended meditation on Crane at the pond and out on its ridge that faces Mateskared. I decided against fire for this sojourn. Fire confuses the rhythm of light and dark and separates you from the unlit surroundings. Like the ego a fire concentrates attention within its delimiting radiance. It sets a boundary between civilization and the wildness that is wilderness. The no-fire decision also ruled out cooking and cut down on gear. Maybe I inherited my father's Luddite, minimalist technology bias. I took a flashlight for safety.

My lack of goal or agenda—other than meditation—rearranged this familiar mountain environment. For the first time I visited the low cliffs on the pond's trail-less side. I had often stared at them from the opposite pond shore, where we would lunch or swim on day trips, or leave the pond for the ridge to forage blueberries while others opted for Crane's summit.

A ledge of the low cliffs where I first chose to meditate was restful but not revelatory. After a couple hours, I returned to my cached my pack and set out onto the ridge, to a favorite tent spot above the valley out of Johnsburg and looking across to Garnet Lake. I think of this favored spot my "shortcut to Colorado." It evokes a profound mountain sense. *"Our place is part of what we are,"* writes poet Gary Snyder, and *"Each place is its own place, forever (eventually) wild."* This is one of mine.

I meditated on the ridge. I watched my mind play until even it got bored and wandered off. I am jealous of Moses' experience of the burning bush. Jealousy is a good motivator for meditating but not for inducing revelation. The result of my peak—or ridge—experience was that I learned to expect nothing of the mountain.

Somewhat crestfallen to have failed to realize any visionary experience, I soon achieved perspective on (a.k.a. "rationalized!") this. God revealed to Moses Godself's name—I Am, or, as it can also be translated, I will be what I will be. In effect, God tells Moses "You will learn my name *as we go along.*" Crane Mountain merely restated my task. It *disciplined* me. I became its disciple.

Crane Mountain from the Cabin Porch

There's no dust to sweep on a mountain. —
Stone House

Seen from Mateskared's porch, Crane Mountain simulates an ever-shifting art exhibition. To visitors who arrive at night, the view and its vagaries come as morning's big surprise. The view is artfully framed, as a viewshed, in a V-shaped notch that partakes of equal parts nature and culture. Part of the V effect is created by the sharp downhill slope of our toe of Height of Land Mountain. An equal part is created by the generous swath of trees cleared out by the electric utility company.

The last electric utility pole out of Bakers Mills runs up onto our property, there to stand beside our outhouse. For 18 years, we were not wired into its intended utility. As a teenager, I photographed its juxtaposition with out outhouse, labeling the scene "Where Progress Meets Privation." My photography aspirations were too short-lived to let the photo's never being published get me down.

Seen from the cabin porch, the treed notch setting up the view hides the power line before it frames the lower of two ridges that are precursors to Crane's ridge and massif.

Another morning effect has to do with haze and creates, through muted visibility and coloration, a natural analog to certain conventions of traditional Oriental landscape painting. Haze mutes the foregrounds of each ridge between Bakers Mills and Crane. That haze thins with elevation, seeming to highlight succeeding ridge lines. The first major ridge line beyond Bakers Mills is close enough to Mateskared that its serrations look like distinct individual trees. This ground-truths the painterly effect. Such a scene may also appear when evening rain follows a hot and humid summer day.

The eyes' attraction to such details makes Crane's massive summit appear to loom higher than it does. Optically, Crane's bulk and visual isolation amplify its ascendance.

At stage left of Crane, Huckleberry Ridge, shaped like a Paul Bunyan-scale meatloaf, reaches just high enough to prevent Crane from enjoying the complete visual hegemony boasted by such volcanic mounts as Baker and Shasta in the Pacific Northwest, and Fuji in Japan, or the not-volcanic Mount McKinley massif in Alaska. Mount McKinley boasts the world's highest vertical relief despite being 6,000 feet shy of the world's tallest peak as measured from mean sea level. McKinley spends much of the summer in clouds. I finally saw the summit clearly after several cloud-hidden days in July 1961. At first, I mistook its snow-clad summit for more clouds.

That Crane evokes such comparison declares its mountain-ness, but topographic relief is relative. British naturalist W. H. Hudson wrote about the Argentine Pampas and how, living there as a child, he loved to stand up on his horse's back. This improved his view over seeming endless flat grasslands. Hudson wrote his classic memoir, *Far Away and Long Ago*, in a down-and-out London boarding-house room. That detail about Hudson's book—my father had me read it in my early teens—gave the title more poignancy.

We were not always so voyeuristic in looking at Crane from Mateskared. In our youths, if one knew where to look, you could peer at Mateskared from Crane. From the end of the ridge on Crane, you could see several structures on Edwards Hill Road. Mateskared looked stranded amidst its rectangle of recovering pasture then. A physicist might object that, if you can see one point from the other, the reverse must be true. But let that physicist ascend to Crane's ridge today and not come down until he or she has pinpointed Mateskared.

Rain just setting in as I wrote the above has now stopped. Did I not know Crane's shape so well, I would doubt I see its faintest outline—and now its top is gone, too? For a few moments, sighting tricks taught at Army night-firing training helped me verify Crane's outline. The trick is to look to the side of the object to be sighted so visual fatigue from staring at a mostly contrast-free shape doesn't blind you.

Crane is fully visible again, the whole of its landscape painting brushed in. But lightning may have persuaded the artist to pack up easel and retreat. Crane is equally on the porch with me at Mateskared as in its own space.

As the great haiku poet Matsuo Bashô reported: "I saw many other things of interest on this mountain, the details of which, however, I refrain from betraying in accordance with the rules I must obey as a pilgrim."

Bashô Walks Onward

"There are times when we feel like taking to the road ourselves," Bashô wrote, "seizing the raincoat lying nearby, or times when we feel like sitting down til our legs take root, enjoying the picture before our eyes." Bashô wrote that—or some editions say his copyist did—in his engaging and enduring *The Narrow Road to the Deep North,* a prose journal peppered with haiku by Bashô, his traveling companion, and sundry hosts and poets en route. The journal is also known as *Back Roads to Far Places.*

I have had several Adirondack travel fantasies over the years, but the most persistent one stems from my frequent readings of Japanese poet Matsuo Bashô's account of his journey. I daydream of walking the Adirondacks by roads from south to north, camping out where nightfall or some attraction beckons, soaking up the scenery, and talking with all and sundry along the way. Nature and culture on the hoof.

Here I go, Bashô —
tent, pen, writing pad, sleep pad—
yacking and scribbling

In adulthood, my concept of wealth changed. Wealth is to have lots of free time and no need to own a car. As down payment toward that elusive end my philosophy has been: Peace on Earth, Goodwill for clothing.

Wayne Wiitanen was one of the original partners with Don Greene, Mary Schaefer, and others in purchasing the old Putnam Farm at the base of Crane Mountain. They bought it for back taxes in the early 1960s. Wayne once told me— I was an impressionable teen then—he thought if you spent four years of honest bumming around you would end up with better preparation for life and work than if you had spent the four years in college.

Wayne had not been a successful undergraduate when he so advised me about college. Some years later, however, he secured a Ph.D. in neurological aspects of vision. He later married Monica Schaefer, Paul and Carolyn's youngest daughter. Wayne is retired now, having worked many years on computer simulations of vision. Even had he followed his own vagrant advice, Wayne's keen intelligence and aptitude for putting early mainframe computers through their paces would have truthed his belief.

By the time Bashô set out on his northern journey, he was a greatly respected elder poet in a culture that held poetry in profound regard. He had invented the haiku form by tinkering with existing forms. Travel would be different for a barefoot poet in our culture. You'd have to go as a journalist, sociologist, or, better yet, TV talk-show recruiter. The poet as world-changer in America is deader than a doornail.

Giving up poetry proved a great career move for Henry Thoreau, even though he had been dead for perhaps 50 years before his prose writing took off. Subsequently, it never slowed down on its way to becoming, as American Renaissance scholar Robert D. Richardson, Jr. has written, "American scripture." Thoreau's fame rests not on an Orphic passage between worlds but on hunkering down for two years beside a suburban Concord, Massachusetts pond. The *whole* world may be too wide a place in which to emplace ourselves. As Emerson acknowledged: "Awed I behold once more / My old familiar haunts. . ."

"There are also times when we feel like taking to the road ourselves, seizing the raincoat lying nearby. . . ." Bashô's image suggests Walt Whitman's "Song of the Open Road" and its pre-automobile cultural perspective. Whitman's road poem actually celebrates nature more than the road itself, that road over which Jack Kerouac and Neal Cassady scurried about to beatify both it and their generation. Nor is the above Bashô's complete sentence: Bashô could also validate Thoreau's two-year stay at Walden Pond. Bashô completes his sentence affirming those times "when we feel like sitting down til our legs take root, enjoying the picture before our eyes."

Alongside the Biblical injunction "Be still and know that I am God," Bashô's declaration scripturally justifies sitting on the Mateskared porch, with Crane Mountain "the picture before our eyes."

Yard rocks, Big Rock, Biggest Rock.

The Language of Life and Death

In life and in death, we belong to God, I tell my sons. We are having one of our obligatory parental monologues as we sit on the cabin porch. My two sons are aged 16 and 13. I call these monologues 'obligatory' because I feel obliged to present them. What the guys want is their breakfast. Their mother is a night person who likes to sleep late on vacation. I am a morning person who likes to get up early on vacation. Night to me is like a prelude to death, a hint or foretaste, a feeling not so much of powerlessness as of do-lessness. Some nights do feel better than others, however.

Nor is each day a God, as Ralph Waldo Emerson would have it. Each day is more like a miniature life cycle. On Sundays down home, we open our church worship service affirming that "In life and in death, we belong to God." So, the week is like a seven-day ritual of daily living and dying. In part, I like to get up early on vacations at Mateskared because, when I was a kid with both parents still alive, we didn't have electricity here. And we didn't—and still don't—allow flames in the upstairs bunkrooms. Night shut down definitively then, the more so because I was a little kid with limited patience for reading by candlelight downstairs. We didn't like to expend flashlight batteries.

As a youngster, your imagination isn't always on your side in the dark. Bedtime was rigidly enforced because my father liked to be alone with my mother, and he didn't sleep late in the morning. What my sons want now is breakfast because I am the breakfast cook. It's a generational thing. That or they want to hear me to say: "You guys can just fix yourself a bowl of cereal this morning."

We end up having most morning monologues on the cabin porch. For me it's where "the view is," and I get up first. For them, it's where you wait for breakfast —or the okay to fix your own. I like okay better than permission. It's like a third-base coach's signal, not an edict from Rome. My mother didn't 'okay' things. She gave you the 'go-ahead.' "You can go ahead and fix yourself a bowl of cold cereal, Edward."

My sons have been taught to calculate how a pot of oatmeal serving four people costs less than two servings of cold cereal and uses no more milk. On the porch, their physical attitude is like they were playing a video game with their hands at parade-rest. Part of this is just waking up. Between worlds, consciousness paints the view soft-featured, like scenic backdrops in old museum dioramas. In my sons' case on vacation mornings, the metaphorical video game is turned off or paused at least.

I prefer the churchly metaphor of life and death. Probably because my own father died before video games were invented. For years, my father didn't allow a TV in our house. When he did relent, he wouldn't allow a TV in the living room. It was in the finished "den" space in our basement.

I imagine each of us can hear 'In life and death, we belong to God' differently. More or less emphasis on the conjunction or the verb and on this or that noun and whether God comes with an initial capital letter or has gender—and if so, which gender?—or not. Or whether this god is a character in a video game, novel, movie, old painting, recurring dream, or ancient stories that even in modern translation have set like concrete.

That my sons understand the intimate relationship between life and death is important to our republican form of democracy and its future. The time that has passed between the death of George Washington and their births is ludicrously short compared to how long dinosaurs lorded it over most of Earth. But in George Washington's day, we didn't have hospitals yet, and now we spend one percent of our Gross Domestic Product each year in hospital Intensive Care Units. Most of this occurs in the last weeks or days of the person's life.

When my older son and I first talked about that statistic, he said, 'Wow, like listen to that language even: Intensive care combined with unit. What does that say?' He was sixteen, but he inherited my father's intuitive grasp of language. "Intensive care" plus "unit" sounds schizoid compared to "In life and in death we belong to God." Actually, when I first said that to my sons that morning, I was relieved Justin didn't pipe up with: 'So what's the difference?' ("Pipe up with" was my mother's expression.) So how would you like to explain the difference between life and death to someone? Even pastors, priests, rabbis, therapists, shrinks, and bartenders often dodge that question.

When Justin and I talked about ICU's and one percent of GDP, our conversation reminded me that Holland spends six percent of its GDP each year on the diking systems that hold back the ocean from the farmland the Dutch created by pushing the ocean farther out into itself. When pictures of our planet came back from outer space, it was pretty apparent that where we live in the Universe should be called the planet 'Water' or 'Ocean' not 'Earth.' Holland pays a six-percent existentialist tax on everything it does, trying to make Earth live up to its minority-surface name.

That's suggestive of combining intensive care with unit or combining no-till with agriculture. Virgil or Hesiod would be as baffled as Hippocrates. Life and death cannot be equally compared with sticking your finger in a dike—unless you are holding back the ocean. And given global climate change, good luck with that.

I haven't figured out how to talk about my own death with Justin and Eric. I don't want it to sound like the old 'You'll miss me when I'm gone' routine. Both might take that as a great straight line and ask: "When are you going?"

I tell them it's no accident that the Romance and Religion sections abut each other in some bookstores. Justin pipes up with 'It's probably alphabetical.' But he knows that's not it. This tells me he's really waking up now. I have only a few more minutes of talking time left. Even the view is pulling out of night mode this time of day — the pseudo lakes between the low hills off toward Crane Mountain shift and then dissipate.

I could explain the phenomenon of orographic winds to Justin and Eric, how hilly or mountainous topography creates its own wind by the daily rising and falling of air masses heated or cooled by the cycle of increasing and decreasing solar heat gain. But that would sound too much like my own father announcing what bird just made that song or call, when what I really wanted to hear about was the birds and the bees, about what it means to love a woman for most of a lifetime or why even best friends sometimes dump on you.

Maybe what I really wanted then was breakfast or the go-ahead to fix my own, as my mother tracked the cabin kitchen of my early life like weather radar.

The photo documents the gathering at the cabin in 1989 to celebrate the 25th Anniversary of The National Wilderness Preservation System Act of 1964. That is Paul Schaefer in the photo addressing the group and standing closest to the cabin. He has some sort of text in his hands, held at navel level.

At the gathering, Anne LaBastille confided to my mother Alice Zahniser that our outhouse—which is basically an ashes-and-hay composting methodology—was the sweetest-smelling outhouse she ever encountered.

Cowshed Dreaming

Who can break from the snares of the world
And sit with me among the white clouds?
    —Cold Mountain

From time to time, people have figured out ways to make money from these "*Adironrocks*." Whether the mining slag by-product of garnet-speckled gravel aggregate for surfacing roads is profitable in itself, I don't know. Garnet has been mined in North River at Barton Mines since 1878. Previously there were substantial Adirondack iron works and limited graphite mining. During World War II, strategic titanium mining took place in the High Peaks region. Titanium was first mined there near Tahawus in 1827.

Throughout my childhood, our cabin activities at Mateskared were irregularly punctuated by the distant blasting *ka-booms* at Barton Mines on the other side of Gore Mountain. The actual garnet mining operations have migrated away from us and closer to the North River, as the Hudson is called this high up toward its High Peaks headwaters. Barton Mines lies within our Thirteenth Lake/Bakers Mills topographic maps. The major activity at the former Barton Mine site is summer tours of its old workings. At the mineral shop, you can buy a variety of garnet pieces plus other minerals and stones from distant points.

Mine tours show you a major old pit, with the large chunks of garnet embedded in its dark, hard-rock walls. Years ago, you could take away such chunks of rock as you could carry. Such prodigality soon pales before the sheer bulk of rock litter strewn about the old operation. The cost and effort of separating the garnet from its host rock reduced profits in Adirondack garnet mining operations.

Hooper Mine, an early garnet operation, lies in our quadrangles near the Garnet Hill Lodge above Thirteenth Lake. Evelyn Schaefer Greene first introduced us to Hooper Mine in the heyday of Justin's youthful interest in rocks and minerals. Evelyn also bushwhacked with us to a tough-to-find, very old small graphite mine near Johnsburg.

The regrowth hardwood forest on the hillside leading up to Hooper Mine shows evidence of relict machinery and other metal artifacts of a former fixed and industrious human presence. The mine itself greets you as an open, roughly rectangular pit with incised cliffs of varying heights on most of three sides. It forms an unnatural amphitheater. Chunks of garnet lie everywhere embedded in standing rock and the slag and scree at the bases of the human-cut cliffs.

Justin likes to visit Hooper Mine every summer and whack the rocks with our masonry hammer. So do I. It renews my optimistic side, which is not reflexively optimistic in the sense that, for example, I am right-handed.

Crystals of garnet look deceptively as though they might pop right out of their rock substrate at you. As Buddhists might say: First thought, best thought. But no such luck. The dull, metallic *thunk* of the masonry hammer's bladed end assailing the rocks is lucky to chip off even a healthy garnet flake. No way do nuggets pop out of the rock. I can't even imagine what hard, hand labor went into early garnet mining. Nor can I quite imagine creating Hooper Mine's pit from its former profile as represented by its current walls' backsides.

On one visit to Hooper Mine, we found a mountain search-and-rescue training session in progress. The rescue litter was lowered on lines anchored to the mine pit's opposing cliff tops. Even given an emergency, I would not relish riding that jerking, sliding litter any more than I would agree to repeat on the Great Escape Amusement Park's Steamin' Demon roller coaster.

Hooper Mine's leveled floor oddly combines dry conditions and pooled water that can't drain from the bedrock floor. All manner of insects and garter snakes are about. No doubt the latter eat the former. A few tree saplings have taken hold, but sparsely. Walking across parts of the pit floor on jumbled slag is like walking stone-cobbled willow and alder flats of Jackson Hole Wyoming's Snake River. What triggers such association? Perhaps the light in sparse sapling stands and the vegetation's aroma.

Or the marsh-like plant with elongated seedheads looking like spiked caterpillars. I associate them with beaver ponds in the Snake River flats. In 1954, using his flyrod, my father and I enticed trout to rise for the seedheads after we lost the two hooks my father brought. A later summer in the Adirondacks, with my fly-tying vise, I lashed similar seedheads to long-shanked streamer fishhooks. Fished like dry flies those lures caught trout. My father had once caught sunfish at Lake Minerva, using rounded white blossoms of a pearly everlasting as bait.

Go in quest of garnet gems at Hooper Mine, and there is no telling what your memory may snag.

Ant Lions, Sand, and the Anthropic Cosmological Principle

For all the boulders they rafted about the Adirondacks to strand as our erratics, massive Ice Age glaciers created a plethora of sand. Road cuts expose vast beds of it. Sand lurks beneath the thin topsoil veneer of Mateskared's sometime garden plot. Sand slopes rise high above town tennis courts at North Creek's Ski Bowl. Slopes stand at such steep angles that large birch trees atop them regularly get undercut. The trees topple as though undercut by a river. Just outside North Creek, another named ski bowl belonging to the Carl Schaefer family, can look like sand dunes stabilized by vegetation. The sand-track lane into Paul Schaefer's brother Carl's place used to mire the occasional car.

Much sand here is so purely sand you can use it to mix mortar without screening or washing. No doubt the sandy subsoil adds to the ground's amenability to growing potatoes. Their outward pressure of growing tissues creates room for the tuber's development. The pressure compacts the soil around the potato—or pushes the potato to the surface. Light-struck there, it will turn its nightshade-family green. Better to hill the rows instead.

Except for the ubiquitous rocks at Mateskared, this sand substrate would make easy digging. Working on the Inn at Gore Mountain, I got a taste of easy digging in pure-bedded sand. The back hoe work on one cellar hole proved slightly off. We had to expand one side with shovels. Digging that sand was like rote martial arts repetitions. The shovel could be inserted in the sand by hand—you did not have to put your foot on it.

The entire motion was *insert shovel, lift shovel, throw sand from pit*. Over and over and over: Rearranging the Ice Age never seemed so simple.

On a day trip my mother and I made north toward the High Peaks area with Paul Schaefer when I was in my teens, we stopped along a river. There on a sandy stretch of its bank I saw my first-ever ant lion operation. The ant lion larvae—they are insects, not spiders—fashioned conical sand pits whose steep sides were pitched at the angle of repose for the sand. The ant lion stations itself below the point of this cone, beneath the sand. If an ant enters the cone, its legs will not readily carry it back out. Instead, they cause the sand grains to collapse downward. The hapless ant is trying to go up the down escalator and makes no progress toward egress. Its furious motion in the sand pit isn't lost on the ant lion—a.k.a. ant devil. Bursting from beneath the sand the ant lion bites the ant and drags it under.

That sandy riverside area had several neat, inverted ant lion cones, whose simple sculptural form was a function of the sand's physical properties. They were built to the steepest angle at which the sand could resist gravity. Continental-scale glaciers and the torrential outwash rivers of their melting retreat were creating sand for the ant lion insect's schemes. This would be equally as miraculous a view of single-purpose cause-and-effect as to suggest that Earth—or Universe, if there be but one—came about primarily to give expression to humans. That is roughly what the Anthropic Cosmological Principle holds!

I say to you ant lions, sand can also be used to mix mortar and concrete or for making glass. Therefore, be not over proud.

In his chapter "Sounds" in *Walden,* Thoreau describes clearing out his small cabin on sunny days to scrub its floor. "When my floor was dirty, I rose early, and, setting all my furniture out of doors on the grass . . . dashed water on the floor, and sprinkled white sand from the pond on it, and then with a broom scrubbed it clean and white. . . ." What this has to do with "Sounds" you may decide. Perhaps Thoreau liked the swishing of the broom whisking sand across his dampened dirt floor. If so, he does not tell us.

The poet E. E. Cummings died in 1962, the centennial of Thoreau's death. Rather than retreat to Walden Pond, Cummings asserted his individualism by aping modern painting with his exploded typography and private poetic grammar. My father introduced me to Cummings' poetry when I was 14 years old. Cummings loved the sound and taste of the words *prurient* and *putresence.* He had to rebel against formidably respectable New England parents. For Cummings *prurient* characterized anyone guilty of reductionist thinking. One prurient Cummings image early impressed me as mightily as contemplating Pleistocene ice sheets: *she came at me like sand caving into a chute. . . .* Not even multi-hour days shoveling sand out of the Inn at Gore Mountain construction pit sufficed to sully that image.

By 1970, the west wall of the Mateskared barn suffered from sagging. The rotting of one of the posts and its supporting sill threatened to neutralize the enduring metal roof's rain protection. Dave Whiteman was a second-generation architecture student, and I was a former construction go-fer and mud mixer. With Dave's know-how, my enthusiasm, and the ubiquitous free rocks scattered about Mateskared, we determined to shore up the barn with a new stone foundation wall on that west side. We did most of the west wall and also built a fieldstone piling to support a new sill on the east wall. Our work still stands despite one longtime crack in our west wall's masonry. No doubt the crack results not from Dave's know-how but from my enthusiasm. We propped up the barn with the Corvair scissors jack to build the wall and insert a new 4x6-inch, rough-sawn pine sill.

Many people who have built stone walls remark on the satisfaction and therapeutic quality of such work. Perhaps an aesthetic pleasure results from the fusion of form and function. Earthy, solid, tangible, tactile work, building fieldstone walls may be an antidote to "civilization and its discontents." Paul Schaefer's brother Carl advised us to use only stones that had naturally weathered exposed to the air. Carl did the masonry work on the Inn at Gore Mountain. I worked as his helper and gopher there and in previous summers in

Schenectady. The streambed behind the barn and the road's edge provided plenty of stones we could move by hand.

To mix the mortar, we built a wood frame covered with hardware cloth to screen sand from the cutbank below the garden plot. On-site rock-and-sand building materials enhanced our satisfaction as our stone wall and piling took shape. They would extend the barn's life. As children my siblings and I played there on rainy cabin days, no doubt to our parents' great relief. After all, they were on vacation, too.

Dave Whiteman later served as a vice president of a large, multi-city architectural firm, headquartered in St. Louis, Missouri. I like to think of our stone wall and fieldstone piling as influential items in Dave's portfolio.

THE NYS WILDERNESS 50ᵀᴴ STEERING COMMITTEE

hereby recognizes

Ed Zahniser

as a historian and spokesman for the American wilderness, writer, editor, essayist and poet who has deepened Americans' understanding of wilderness in their lives, and within the greater community of life.

May 7, 2014

Adirondack Wild: Friends of the Forest Preserve & the Nelson A. Rockefeller Institute of Government, in cooperation with the SUNY College of Environmental Science and Forestry and NYS Department of Environmental Conservation.

Wilderness Act 50th Anniversary, 2014

The world contains many things that exist but cannot be collected and put someplace—the set of complex numbers, gravity, dreams. Wildness is similar and we are not very clear about how to preserve it. — Jack Turner

Howard Zahniser died four months before the 1964 Wilderness Act became law 50 years ago September 3, 2014. Zahnie was the chief architect of, and lobbyist for this landmark Act, which created our now 111-million-acre National Wilderness Preservation System. He did his Basic Training in Grassroots Wilderness Advocacy with Paul Schaefer in and around the Adirondacks beginning in 1946.

Paul Schaefer lived by letterheads. He had a double fistful over the years, specific to conservation causes. I was born in 1945. So was Paul's letterhead group Friends of the Forest Preserve, formed to fight what became known as the Black River Wars. The issue was the threat to build several dams in western New York on "Forever Wild" Forest Preserve lands in the Western Adirondacks.

My late sisters Esther and Karen and my brother Matt and I would often address each other as "Dear Friends of the Forest Preserve." Matt and I still do so on occasion. Today the organization is Adirondack Wild: Friends of the Forest Preserve.

When I first read James Glover's *A Wilderness Original: The Life of Bob Marshall*, it reminded me that many family friends I grew up taking for granted as my father's national conservation associates had been recruited by New Yorker Bob Marshall in his frequent travels. Marshall's cohorts and co-founders of The Wilderness Society included Benton MacKaye, Bernard Frank, Harvey Broome, Aldo Leopold, and Ernest Oberholtzer. They carried on Marshall's wilderness work as The Wilderness Society after Marshall died at age 38 in 1939.

MacKaye, Frank, and Leopold were trained foresters, as was Marshall, who also held a PhD in plant physiology from The Johns Hopkins University. Broome was a lawyer for the Tennessee Valley Authority, where MacKaye and Frank worked as foresters. Also helping with Marshall's early Wilderness Society work were his personal recruits Sigurd Olson and Ernest Oberholtzer, advocates for what is today the Boundary Waters Canoe Area Wilderness in Minnesota, and Olaus and Margaret E. "Mardy" Murie, who played crucial roles in the creation of the Arctic National Wildlife Refuge in Alaska.

Bob Marshall inspired wilderness advocacy not only for federal public lands but also for the Adirondack wilderness. He spent youthful summers at the Marshall family camp near Saranac Lake. In July 1932, three years before The Wilderness Society was organized, Bob Marshall ran into a young Paul Schaefer atop Mount Marcy. Schaefer was photographing ravages of forest fires caused by careless logging of Adirondack High Peaks forests *above* the elevations that loggers had assured Bob Marshall and others that they would not cut.

Paul Schaefer was doing what *his* conservation mentor John Apperson said we must do. Stand on the land you want to save. Take pictures so the public sees what is at stake. John Apperson's rallying cry was "We Will Wake Them Up!" Paul would practice exactly that for more than fifty years of wildlands advocacy. Atop Mount Marcy, not far above Verplanck Colvin's Lake Tear of the Clouds, Marshall captured Paul Schaefer's wild imagination. Marshall called for wilderness advocates to band together, which led to The Wilderness Society's birth in 1935.

In 1946, 14 years after his peak experience with Bob Marshall, Paul Schaefer recruited Howard Zahniser to defend Adirondack forest preserve wilderness lands. Apperson and Schaefer had showed their documentary film about the dam-building threats to western Adirondack forest preserve lands at the February 1946 North American Wildlife Conference in New York City. Zahnie had gone to work for The Wilderness Society in September 1945, and had attended the wildlife conferences for many years in his prior work with the U.S. Bureau of Biological Survey and later the U.S. Fish and Wildlife Service. After the presentation by Apperson and Schaefer, my father told Schaefer The Wilderness Society would help defend the western Adirondacks against dams in what became known as the Black River Wars.

When they took up the gauntlet in 1946 to block the series of dams was widely deemed a lost cause. But Schaefer and Zahnie went from town to town in western New York, testifying at public hearings, meeting with news people and outlets, and identifying and cultivating local advocates of saving the wilderness and wildlands.

Zahnie also brought natural resource experts and representatives of eight national conservation organizations from Washington, D.C. to New York to testify against the dams. So Paul Schaefer was Zahnie's mentor in sticking with lost causes, too. As Olaus Murie later said—and this is my all-time favorite comment about my father—"Zahnie has unusual tenacity in lost causes." That was a New York State skill.

The next summer, 1947, The Wilderness Society governing council voted to pursue some form of more permanent protection for wilderness. That 1947 vote set the stage for the 1964 Wilderness Act.

The administrative classifications of wildlands that Bob Marshall and Aldo Leopold had won to protect wilderness on the federal, national forests were proving ephemeral. A housing boom followed World War II's end in 1945. Federal bureaucrats immediately started de-classifying administratively designated wilderness areas to exploit their timber, minerals, and hydropower.

Under Schaefer's tutelage, Zahnie dove into the Black River Wars in New

York State in 1946. Zahnie's federal government public relations work had taught him the machinations of multi-media publicity. But from and with Paul Schaefer in the Adirondacks, Zahnie learned firsthand the art of grass roots organizing and stumping for wilderness. Paul Schaefer built a statewide coalition of hunters, anglers, and other conservationists. He held this coalition together by the strength of his personality for half a century.

This is why we can call the Adirondacks and Catskills "where wilderness preservation began." The epic early 1950s fight against the Echo Park Dam proposed *inside* Dinosaur National Monument in Utah would result in building the first-ever national conservation coalition. Then, having defeated the dam project by 1955, Zahnie and the Sierra Club's David Brower put their coalition to work for the legislation that would become the 1964 Wilderness Act.

Zahnie and David Brower led the Echo Park Dam fight. At the 1994 National Wilderness Conference, Brower told my wife Christine and me that Zahnie was his mentor in the practical technics of conservation advocacy. This puts David Brower in the direct line of Adirondack wilderness advocacy mentoring by Bob Marshall, John Apperson, and Paul Schaefer.

In 1953 Zahnie gave a speech in Albany, New York to a committee of the New York State legislature. This was my father's first major public formulation of the wilderness idea. His topic was the remarkable record of the people of the Empire State in preserving in perpetuity a great resource of wilderness on their public lands. The speech was titled "New York's Forest Preserve and Our American Program for Wilderness."

In August 1996, David Gibson and Ken Rimany, Paul Schaefer's grandson David Greene, and my brother Matt Zahniser and I and our four sons backpacked across the High Peaks to commemorate the 50th anniversary of the 1946 trip made by Schaefer, Ed Richard, and Zahnie. It remains crucially important to speak clearly and strongly for this unparalleled legacy of wildness—in the Adirondacks and nationally—that we love and cherish. And only astute wilderness stewardship can put the *forever* in a "wilderness forever future."

Congress declared the intent of the National Wilderness Preservation System Act to be "for the permanent good of the whole people . . ." —and this by a 1964 House of Representatives vote of 373 to 1. Isn't that amazing? And the earlier Senate vote was 78 to 12.

Wilderness and wildness are integral to what Wendell Berry calls " the circumference of mystery." Wilderness and wildness are integral to what the poet Denise Levertov calls "the Great Web." Wilderness and wildness are integral to what the Reverend Dr. Martin Luther King Jr. calls "our inescapable network of mutuality." Wilderness and wildness are integral to what God describes to Job as the "circle on the face of the deep," to the bio-sphere, to our circle of life, to our full community of life on Earth that derives its existence from the Sun.

The prophetic call of wilderness is not to escape the world. The prophetic call of wilderness is to encounter the world's essence. John Hay calls wilderness the "Earth's immortal genius." Gary Snyder calls wilderness "the planetary intelligence." Wilderness calls us to renewed kinship with all of life. In Aldo Leopold's words, *"we will enlarge the ethical boundaries of the community—we will live out a land ethic—only as we feel ourselves a part of the same community."*

By securing a national policy of restraint and humility toward natural conditions and wilderness character, the Wilderness Act prompts Americans toward a sociopolitical step to secure a land ethic that enlarges the boundaries of our human community.

Preserving wilderness and wildness is about recognizing the limitations of our desires and the limitations of our capabilities within nature. But nature really is this all-encompassing community—including humans—that Aldo Leopold characterized simply as "the land." In preserving designated wilderness, we put a small percentage of the land outside the scope of our trammeling influence.

President Lyndon B. Johnson signed the Wilderness Act into law on September 3, 1964. My mother Alice Zahniser stood in our father's place at the White House Rose Garden signing, and President Johnson gave her a pen he used. The future of American wilderness lies in continued concerted advocacy by spirited people intent on seeing our visionary legacy of thinking—and feeling—about wilderness and wildness taken up by each new generation.

Howard Zahniser said that in preserving wilderness, we take some of the precious ecological heritage that has come down to us from the eternity of the past, and we have the boldness to project it into the eternity of the future. If you are looking for good work, you will find no better work than to be a conduit for those two eternities. Go forth, do good, tell the stories, and keep it wild.

Adapted from a talk by Ed Zehneiser at the 50th Anniversary Celebration of Wilderness, held at the Kelly Adirondack Center of Union College in Schenectady, NY, May 8, 2014.

Coda: The Scale of Our Desires

Prophets do not come from cities, promising riches and store clothes.
They have always come from the wilderness, stinking of goats
and running with lice and telling of a different sort of treasure.
— Andrew Lytle

Wholly Holy Other

During a conference presentation in Oregon, philosopher and historian of the wilderness idea Max Oelschlaeger cited my father as an example of an environmentalist with religious motivation. Wildness as surrogate sacred or Holy? Wildness as confronting otherness? Some theologians position the category of the sacred, or the Holy, as total Otherness. Wholly Holy Other.

Yahweh courts the Israel of post-Egyptian servitude for 40 years' wandering exodus in non-anthropocentric wilderness. Forty years? To spend fully one and one-third generations on so small a space of map without base camps, you would need to *wander* in carefully executed spirals, like early models of DNA gathered around a chromosome. *Exodus* as synchronized swimming in the desert. With model leave-no-trace wilderness-use management, Yahweh feeds the Israelites on manna. This 'name' does not mean 'bread' and is not even a noun. It's an exclamation: "What is it?!?"

The Exodus wilderness story is the story of the molding of a covenantal culture in that desert wilderness space abjectly free of the world of constructs and artifacts. The nascent covenantal nation Israel had to defamiliarize itself to put an end to its body-mind captivity.

Jesus of Nazareth reduced the wilderness theme—in what would become the Christian New Testament—to 40 days. Rather than bother with manna, Jesus fasted on the mountain. His cousin, John the Baptist, was in line for the high priesthood, but chose instead to enter the wilderness. There, outside the world of constructs and artifacts, he took the prophet's stance.

Wildness as Other. To be in a landscape not shaped by *Homo faber*, Humankind the maker, is revelatory both of essential human nature and the nature of the other. My father referred to this otherness as "the whole community of life on Earth . . ." to which he would add ". . . of which we are a part."

My wife Christine never met my father. He died three years before she and I met. As I read to her once from a speech my father had delivered 40 years earlier, she interjected: "What religious language!" *Perpetuity. Out of the eternity of the past and into the eternity of the future. The boldness to presume upon the eternal. We who live but our three score years and ten.*

The Wilderness Act's vocabulary admits only of *perpetuity* not *eternity*.

In his appeals to protect wilderness in the late 1950s and up to his death in May 1964, Zahnie eventually coaxed his pitch about wilderness toward more human-centered and utilitarian language. Ours is a consensus politics of competing interest groups. The conservation movement had only just begun to use rigorous language of science in its advocacy. Rachel Carson had showed how to do that with her *Silent Spring*, with its 1962 unmasking of the hazards of pesticides. Carson's rigorous science called them out as dangerous biocides, not targeted pesticides. Zahnie and Carson had briefly worked together for the U.S. Fish and Wildlife Service. With Sigurd F. Olson, Zahnie helped Carson with publishing contacts for her book.

David Brower would muster engineering reports to rebut the Bureau of Reclamation's own claims about the safety and evaporation rates of the proposed Echo Park Dam scheme in the mid-1950s. The environmental movement was not yet invented then but was a-borning.

In the 1930s, Robert Marshall had posed the need for wilderness preservation as a minority rights issue. Thoreau's essay "Walking" proposes to "speak a word for Nature, for absolute freedom and wildness"—"because the preacher, baker, butcher, and almost anyone else will talk up civilization."

Wilderness, wildness: now they are even more a minority as landscapes than in the time of Bob Marshall, who died at age 38 in 1939. Marshall himself was a border figure. He played Lewis and Clark in unmapped terrain. Thoreau imagined small brooks as the Mississippi River, the Orinoco. Paul Schaefer searched for the unmapped Nate Davis Pond in the 1960s.

Defamiliarization: Mateskared now rests amidst a shrinking ecotone, a closing edge between civilization and the wilderness.

Lilac Time

*Still grows the vivacious lilac a generation after
the door and lintel and the sill are gone, unfolding its sweet-scented
flowers each spring, to be plucked by the musing traveler.*
— Henry David Thoreau

A favorite snippet of British poetry my father liked to read aloud at our dining room table in the Washington, D.C. suburbs began: "Come down to Kew in lilac time, / It isn't far from London." His intense delight in the piece showed in how he would dip one shoulder and lean headlong into his small, family audience of five during a recitation. He used his body to punctuate his public speaking about wilderness, too, with his bob-and-weave guided walk-through of rhetorical emphases.

"Come down to Kew in lilac time . . ." There are certain words a lifetime loads with meaning. *Lilac* was one. Think of Walt Whitman's "When lilacs last in the dooryard bloomed . . ." Its poignancy suggests an aura of spring, but also its heavy, 19th-Century scent of death and dying. It was Whitman's eulogy for the assassinated President Abraham Lincoln.

At Mateskared, the lilacs usually bloom in May. We have a now scraggly stand that was planted around 1939 by Harold and Pansy Allen. It was a subsistence farm then. The lilacs still hold forth in "the dooryard," between the woodshed attached to our cabin and the sugar maple tree above the small barn.

My wife Christine and I witnessed these lilacs' blooming in the five-month period we lived at Mateskared on our delayed honeymoon in 1970, after my draft-induced military service during the Viet Nam era. The beginnings of a great hope: Lilacs and spring. Just *whose* lifetime has loaded *lilac* with this peculiar meaning is not entirely clear to me now. Was it my father's or mine, mine or my father's? Either/or; both/and, perhaps?

What may be the largest cellar dent uphill from Mateskared can only be located now by the incongruously large lilac bushes growing otherwise anomalously in the recovering forest there. The late great New York state conservationist Paul Schaefer cited these lilacs in his August 13, 1946 letter to explain to my father the location of the woodlot that Harold and Pansy wanted to sell along with the smaller plot of land their house sat on.

The woodlot lay just above where the old road makes its right-angled turn toward the community of Sodom to all but disappear now in recovering woodlands. Nature re-enclosing culture: these spreading uphill lilacs, these planted dreams of the human dooryard, these cultivated dreams of an agricultural way of life in a harsh and hilly place. No matter that so-called "economic agriculture" had migrated westward by Thoreau's time, to where river valleys may boast of topsoil up to 20 feet deep. Next to Mateskared the topsoil is some three inches deep. Underneath are rocks and sand. Lots of rock. Enormous amounts of sand.

When I was very young, my whole family went up by those lilacs and their cellar dent—still at the edge of their former clearing then. Our mission: to cut hay to make "hay tick" mattresses by stuffing the mattress shells my mother sewed up for the purpose. I remember feeling a grand sense of our family "making do" together in that practical task. And why feather the nests of Mateskared mice over the coming winter with the bought, commercial mattress batting?

My father's patron saint of wildness, Henry Thoreau, wrote often about the many cellar dents near Concord, Massachusetts. A hundred years before Mateskared's retreat from rurality toward wildness began, Concord-area "economic agriculture" had already headed westward. *"Still grows the vivacious lilac a generation after the door and lintel and the sill are gone, unfolding its sweet- scented flowers each spring, to be plucked by the musing traveler,"* Thoreau noted in *Walden*. My father read Thoreau's book several times throughout his adult life. Thoreau noted, too, how eerily and emotionally similar cellar dents were to the dents that settle over a freshly dug grave.

Thoreau knew fresh-dug graves intimately. Dreams of livelihood lay dashed in cellar dents. The dream of life itself lies dashed in grave dents. His brother John Thoreau died at age 27 in 1842. Thoreau nursed him right through the final horrors of his death by lockjaw—from a razor cut sustained from shaving. Thoreau's first book *A Week on the Concord and Merrimack Rivers* was his brother John's express memorial. It was to write that book that Thoreau repaired to Emerson's newly purchased woodlot out by Walden Pond.

Then there was the grave dent of Emerson's young first wife, Ellen. She died of the tuberculosis that would also claim Henry Thoreau at age 42. The Emersons had been married just 17 months then. Emerson's grief was so great, so lasting, that eight years later his second wife, Lidian, suggested that they name their first daughter Ellen.

And then the grave of Emerson's young son, little Waldo, dead of scarlatina at age five, barely two weeks after Thoreau's brother John had died of lockjaw.

Cellar dents and grave dents, and those lilacs that last in the dooryard bloomed.

On April 29, 1964, my father wrote a letter by hand to Paul Schaefer and invoked the lilacs in Mateskared's own dooryard. He reported briefly to Paul on the (final) hearings just completed on the legislation that in five months would become the 1964 Wilderness Act. He told Paul how he had survived the hearings, but barely, breaking out in sweats during his testimony. His letter alluded to his earlier, long-standing hopes that he would have "a post-wilderness bill period of writing." Now he didn't think that was to be.

And wouldn't it be wonderful, he asked Paul, if we could see again together the blooming of the lilacs at Mateskared? The lilacs would have bloomed in two weeks or so. My father died six days after writing the letter to Paul.

Lilacs: I think now my father invoked the lilacs to share with Paul, however less than point-blank, that he was dying. In the course of writing my father's biography, *Wilderness Forever: Howard Zahniser and the Path to the Wilderness Act*, environmental historian Mark Harvey tracked down three letters my father wrote that same day, April 29. One he wrote to my sister Karen, away at college then. One he wrote to his sister Helen and her husband Lee Snyder. The third was the letter to Paul Schaefer.

"Your father *knew* he was dying then," Mark said.

One's world collapses inward with the closing in of death foreknown. It seems utterly appropriate that of so few hand-penned declarations, oblique except in collective retrospect, one was this small, lilac-nuanced testament to his longtime conservation-action mentor and friend Paul Schaefer, to our family cabin Mateskared, and to the forever-wild Adirondacks.

"So this was Bob Marshall's country. No wonder he loved it so."

Ed with father Howard.

The World, Beauty, Pattern, and Order

You preserve mostly by inaction.
— *Freeman Tilden*

Every fact is also an act of desire.
— *Jeanette Winterson*

Cellars dent. Graves dent. Stones rot. Only the chants remain: In the David Ferry translation of the *Odes*, Book Three, Roman poet Horace (65 to 8 BCE) proclaims:

> *Today I have finished a work outlasting bronze*
> *And the pyramids of ancient royal kings.*
> *The North Wind raging cannot scatter it*
> *Nor can the rain obliterate this work,*
> *Nor can the years, nor can the ages passing.*
> *Some part of me will live and not be given*
> *Over into the hands of the death goddess.*

Thoreau did not say that we preserve wildness. He said: ". . . in Wildness is the preservation of the World." Wildness preserves us, the World, *Kosmos* in Greek, where it means not only World, but Beauty, Pattern, and Order, too. One of my father's favorite texts was from *Walden*:

"We can never have enough of Nature. We must be refreshed by the sight of inexhaustible vigor, vast and Titanic features, the sea-coast with its wrecks, the wilderness with its living and its decaying trees, the thundercloud, and the rain which lasts three weeks and produces freshets. We need to witness our own limits transgressed, and some life pasturing freely where we never wander."

Wildness preserves us. "It is in vain to dream of a wildness distant from ourselves . . . ." Thoreau wrote in his journal in August 1856. "I shall never find in the wilds of Labrador any greater wilderness than in some recess in Concord."

I think my father *knew* that—"in some recess"—at Mateskared.

It does no good to try to hide the obvious paradox: My report to you of the process of bonding to this place Mateskared has held forth both a familiarity hazarding nostalgia and the defamiliarization implicit in an exodus experience. I am consoled only by the fact that those who study in exquisite detail the extensive literature of our "sense of place" often report back somewhat paradoxically. "If we idealize the sense of place as a panacea for the disaffections of modern uprootedness," writes Lawrence Buell, for example, "we run almost as great a risk of cultural narcissism as when we accept the myth of place-free, objective inquiry."

That is not an entirely satisfactory explanation, either. But it signals nostalgia's danger: You could run to Mateskared as to the shopping mall.

Or perhaps the fundament of the firmament is that, as so many religious traditions teach, you cannot save yourself by setting out to save yourself. You can only save yourself through accepting and serving the self-willed-ness of the Other. No doubt that sounds like preachment, but it means only to preface how Thoreau proved-out his word *wildness* etymologically as 'self-willed-ness.'

The Wild is that which is self-willed, whether human individual, political system, or today's ecosystem in what philosopher and magician David Abram calls "the more-than-human world." It was this 'Wildness' in Thoreau's essay "Resistance to Civil Government" that inspired Mahatma Gandhi's self-rule movement in India and helped to shape the prophetic dream of the Reverend Dr. Martin Luther King Jr. Much of *Walden*, a book so often approached as the chronicle of an escape, instead hammers away at provoking social reflection, at provoking social change.

Walden neglects to report this incident, but Thoreau's journal records it: The Concord-area Underground Railroad group met at his hut at Walden Pond. Thoreau was known among his Concord neighbors—among those who would know about such illegal and necessarily secret things—as the person most active locally in this human freedom movement. The *Boston Globe* newspaper recently editorialized the Underground Railroad as "an infrastructure of conscience." Not only illegal and secret but also therefore without either rails or payroll, this 'railroad's' operation left virtually no tracks on landscape or on paper. Now its wildness must be preserved "at the frayed edges of national memory," as the *Boston Globe* graphically editorialized, by "the radical act of remembering."

I prefer to harbor my fugitive self just now in the comparative safety of thinking of Mateskared as neighbor to wilderness. I may still have years enough left to screw up my nerve and front the fact of Mateskared as neighboring wildness. I hope so.

I have sat long and often on the porch at Mateskared, staring at the same view my father and mother and, now, departed sibling sisters Esther and Karen stared at. I am beginning to know now something my father and mother had wanted to tell me about Thoreau, and about wilderness and wildness—that is to say, about life itself: You cannot add life to a life that is truly life. Somehow that calls us equally to advocate preservation of wilderness and wildness and to advocate social justice. The scale of our desires too often works to marginalize nature and many fellow and sister humans, too.

I wish I could tell you that the advent of my knowing this involved a moment of dramatic epiphany. It did not. I was reading Bill McKibben's book *The Age of Missing Information*. In it, McKibben tries to differentiate between real information and what today we are told is information. Real information would be that cultural complex of customs, techniques, rituals, orders, and stories that would make it so difficult to fit into a viable, working village, simply because *there would be so much to learn*. McKibben contrasts such real information with what passes for information today, in something like the global advertising slogan: "Coke adds life." In one African language the slogan reads, he says: "Coke brings your ancestors back from the dead."

Or how else *could* we add to life?

Like most important meanings in my life Mateskared enfolds itself to paradox. To become familiar with Mateskared has been a long, slow defamiliarizing with the world of constructs and artifacts. "I imagine it to be some advantage to live a primitive and frontier life—though in the midst of an outward civilization," Thoreau confided to his journal. The key word may not be *primitive*, or *frontier*, or *civilization*. The key word may be Thoreau's verb *imagine*.

Or the key phrase may be "in the midst of an outward civilization."

Wouldn't that be the "sense of place," the midst? Mateskared has been for me this midst place—perched between civilization and the wilderness. I suppose I could have come up thinking of Mateskared as neighbor to civilization, rather than neighbor to wilderness. But the meaning of Mateskared for me is not only paradoxical but parabolical.

I think of the parable Jesus told about the Good Samaritan. It is so easy to get caught up in the intricacies of the political, ecclesiastical, and sociological data compressed into this small story that we forget why Jesus told it in the first place. He was responding to the sophistry of the question: Well, then, who is my neighbor? The question had been asked by a churchman, let's say.

The churchman has just witnessed the reduction of his culture-forming Ten Commandments to just two. Love God . . . and love your neighbor as yourself. Ultimately, in good Jesus fashion, the questioner must answer his own question at the tale's end. Who then was the better neighbor to the beaten and robbed victim?

The one who showed mercy.

Not preachment but preface: One definition of a parable is "a story whose meaning cannot be exhausted in its telling."

Howard Zahniser and Paul Schaefer made Mateskared a locus of mercy directed uphill, toward the wilderness. Call such mercy 'conservation' for now. In July 1948, Paul declared that the "highest use" of the valley of the South Branch of the Moose River was "preservation in its natural state." Paul's assessment lay so far out of the mainstream then, it must have sounded like a jeremiad from deeper time.

In fact, it came instead from future time. It was Paul's prophetic stance asserted in and for the wilderness.

In the early 1970s, Paul Schaefer would recall his first backpack trip into Beaver Lake in the Higley Mountain country in May 1945. It was the very country threatened by the dam proposals that Paul and Zahnie would come together the next year to fight:

"I stood there in awe at the perfection of nature around me. Then came the sudden realization that all of this might soon be lost forever: the great forest reduced to a cemetery of stumps; the rich lush forest floor alternately drowned and dry; and the music of the river stilled. Even as I stood silent on this spot, a deer emerged from the shadows of the forest to drink in a sunlit pool. Just upstream, a trout leaped for a fly.

"Here was wilderness—solitude, serenity, and peace!

"Who, having seen such moments, could abandon such country to the fate we foresaw?"

It came down to a matter of scale. "Any spiritual tradition worthy of the name teaches the diminishment of desire," Jack Turner writes in *The Abstract Wild*, "and it is desire in all its forms—simple greed, avarice, hoarding, the will to power, the will to truth, the rush of population growth, the craving for control—that fuels the destruction of our once-fair planet. I believe that virtually all problems are problems of scale, and I know, to the degree that I know anything, that desire usually drives us to adopt scales that are inappropriate to their subjects. This is as true for emotion and forestry as it is for hunting and global economics."

When the National Audubon Society decided to get serious about advocating justice toward the environment, it hired Charles Callison as its chief political strategist. "Paul Schaefer has probably come as close to seeing all of [the Adirondack Mountains] than anyone ever did," Callison wrote, "and worked harder to save it . . ." Callison labored side by side for wilderness preservation with both my father and with Paul for many, many years. He cited Paul's "love for a wild land and his unflagging determination to preserve it." Unflagging determination. Paul took up the gauntlet of the Black River Wars when the dams were considered a done deal and the situation hopeless, the war lost before begun.

"Zahniser as an advocate was unfailingly polite and well tempered—but relentless," historian Stephen Fox wrote in his book *John Muir and His Legacy: The American Conservation Movement*.

"Who, having seen such moments, could abandon such country to the fate we foresaw?"

Stephen Fox points out a 'balanced judgment' my father once made about the epic antagonists Gifford Pinchot, a utilitarian conservationist, and John Muir, a preservationist. Fox writes that this incident "suggested one of Zahniser's finest qualities. He had firm opinions of his own, but in dealing with other conservationists he was courteous, good-humored, diplomatic, ecumenical, an earnest advocate who also listened well. During the fractious campaigns of the 1950s, he was the common denominator, holding the center together and in touch with everyone, implacable but imperturbable."

Which is to say that Mateskared was and is "the midst place."

Mateskared is like an ecotone, an edge, the boundary between civilization and the wilderness. Ecotones support more diversity of life than either of the environments whose coming-together defines them as such. In much of the American West, riparian edges, often extremely narrow corridors of green, burgeoning life that line rivers and streams, make up less than two percent of the land surface. Nevertheless, they contain the lion's share of the land's biological diversity.

When Paul Schaefer lured Zahnie to the Adirondack frays in 1946, Paul was inviting unbeknownst the ecological cast of mind into New York State conservation politics. It was the cast of mind that the people who formed the nucleus of the Wilderness Society had had implanted in them by Aldo Leopold, Olaus Murie, and Edward Preble, my father's mentor for whom I am named. "Philosophically," Fox writes, "the ecological cast of mind implied treating all conservation issues as aspects of a single problem; practically it meant cooperating with other groups."

Mateskared was the midst place for conservation cooperation.

". . . all conservation issues as aspects of a single problem:" "Three decades have passed now," Lawrence Buell wrote in the 1990s, "since the publication of Rachel Carson's *Silent Spring* and the passage of the Wilderness Act, which marked the full-fledge emergence of environmentalism as a topic of public concern in America."

". . . aspects of a single problem." Stephen Fox writes that my father "looked like a misplaced librarian, bald, bespectacled, and bookish." Free time in any town or city meant a chance to root out and explore its secondhand book shops. "His enormous personal collection of nature books was eventually donated to the Conservation Center of the Denver Public Library, the main repository of historical materials on conservation. The books reflected the man: Zahniser had one of the sharpest, best-stocked minds in conservation."

As wilderness was for wildness, so secondhand book shops were for civilization. A midst place . . . aspects of a single problem: his interest in Dante, Blake, Thoreau, and the Book of Job. It was and is a matter of scale, which may be the ultimate paradox of wildness. The "absolute freedom" Thoreau asserts for wildness in his essay "Walking" also demands that we know well our human limits.

Where were *you*, God asks Job exasperatedly after Job demands an audience with the creator? Where were you when I drew a circle on the face of the deep?

In *The Age of Missing Information,* McKibben reflects on our human scale from his perch on Crow Mountain: "The consumer society, exemplified by television, is obsequious in its attentions, and promises you all happiness. Whereas the mountain is indifferent. It promotes a brand of existentialism—it's hard, sitting on a mountain, to think that there's some great and exalted and sensible reason for your presence on this planet. But it's a joyful existentialism, because we so clearly can fit in—because the world in which we're inexplicably thrown is magnificent, sweet. It's within our power, too, to leave some of it alone. To witness its rightness. That may be our real importance—as the only creatures who can so fully comprehend how correct and harmonious the world is."

Sometimes at Mateskared I get the feeling I have sat on that same mountain. Sometimes I think I see its shape emerging with the dawn, with flat-topped pockets of morning mist caught like lakes nested in its lowest foothills.

"We deeply need the humility to know ourselves as the dependent members of a great community of life," Zahnie wrote, " . . . to recognize [our] littleness, to sense dependence and interdependence, indebtedness, and responsibility." That credo summarizes both his supreme optimism about America's wilderness preservation movement and his abject disappointment with our use of the atomic bombs in World War II. It all comes down to a sense of scale, to restraint, to the diminishment and limitations of desire, to the scale of our desires.

My mother distinctly recalls that the news of the bombs being dropped on Japan made my father physically ill for several days. It was certainly no accident that Zahnie left secure federal government employment in late 1945 to go to work for a fledgling movement whose root agenda was to redefine progress—this time from an ecological cast of mind.

Aldo Leopold had said his land ethic concept came down to "widening the boundaries of the community."

Mateskared, a midst place and neighbor to wilderness. What better place than an ecotone from which to cast one's net in the wildest hope of widening the boundaries of the community?

Epilogue: Reciprocity, by David Abram

It is the salmon, in their sad, eloquent way, that are instructing us to take down the dams, and we would do well to acknowledge their active influence in all this. For our own health, I suspect, we need to accept that there are other animate forces in the world besides ourselves and our technologies. We need to acknowledge that humans are not the only active agents in this earthly world—that there are other kinds, other shapes, other styles of active agency.

Alice and Howard Zahniser.